Sandcastles Don't Last Forever

Biblical Keys to Earn Rewards that Stand the Test of Time

Milton Goh

Dedication

One day when I was singing praises to God, an image floated up in my spirit: a big and beautiful sandcastle being washed away by the waves from the sea. God was teaching me the futility of holding tightly onto worldly possessions because like the sandcastle, they won't last, and one day will cease to exist.

He taught me from His word to focus on Him and by doing so, I would reap great heavenly rewards at the final judgment - Rewards that will last forever, and can't be destroyed or stolen.

It is my prayer that the revelations in this book will help you to live with a focus on eternity, fulfill your God-given calling in life, be happier, and to accumulate more heavenly rewards to your account.

As with any reading any book, read it and after that study the Scriptures for yourself to see if the Holy Spirit in you bears witness with what I'm writing.

I would like to dedicate this book firstly to my Lord Jesus Christ for being the Source of all good things in my life. Secondly, to my wife Emilee and daughter Maeleth for being the most important people in my life who also love Jesus. Finally, to all my patrons on Patreon who make the dream of writing Christian content full-time for Jesus more and more possible by helping to fund this ministry. Special shoutout to the exceedingly generous patrons: Terence, Shanice and Sene. God bless you and Jesus loves you!

Table of Contents

Good Investment Advice from a Trillionaire in the Bible

Regarding weighing the worth of godly versus worldly pursuits, we all need to read the words of one of the wisest and wealthiest mortal men who ever lived - King Solomon. When God came to him in a dream and asked what would he like God to give to him, Solomon asked for wisdom, and this pleased God.

"I have also given you that which you have not asked, both riches and honor, so that there will not be any among the kings like you for all your days." (1 KINGS 3:13 WEB)

Solomon was not only blessed with great wisdom, but also wealth and honor. Sources estimate his net worth to be more than US$2 Trillion, making him one of the wealthiest men who ever lived.

Solomon in his pursuit for secular wisdom apart from God gave himself over to every fleshly desire in the world. Take note that this is one of the richest men ever that we are talking about, so he really had access to the best that the world could offer.

"Whatever my eyes desired, I didn't keep from them. I didn't withhold my heart from any joy, for my heart rejoiced because of all my labor, and this was my portion from all my labor. Then I looked at all the works that my hands had worked, and at the labor that I had labored to do; and behold, all was vanity and a chasing after wind, and there was no profit under the sun." (ECCLESIASTES 2:10-11 WEB)

After trying everything, his conclusion was that everything was vain, empty and futile - they couldn't satisfy him. Here's another piece of wisdom from him for people who love money.

"He who loves silver shall not be satisfied with silver; nor he who loves abundance, with increase: this also is vanity. When goods increase, those who eat them are increased; and what advantage is there to its owner, except to feast on them with his eyes? The sleep of a laboring man is sweet, whether he eats little or much; but the abundance of the rich will not allow him to sleep. There is a grievous evil which I have seen under the sun: wealth kept by its owner to his harm. Those riches perish by misfortune, and if he has fathered a son, there is nothing in his hand. As he came out of his mother's womb, naked shall he go again as he came, and shall take nothing for his labor, which he may carry away in his hand. This also is a grievous evil, that in all points as he came, so shall he go. And what profit does he have who labors for the wind? All his days he also eats in darkness, he is frustrated, and has sickness and wrath." (ECCLESIASTES 5:10-17 WEB)

He wrote that worldly riches don't satisfy or make one happy. Instead, the greed for more consumes a person and makes him sleepless, frustrated, sick, angry and unhappy. This advice comes from a man who is very qualified to give it. So the important question is, what does Solomon conclude to be the most worthy pursuit in life?

"This is the end of the matter. All has been heard. Fear God and keep his commandments; for this is the whole duty of man. For God will bring every work into judgment, with every hidden thing, whether it is good, or whether it is evil." (ECCLESIASTES 12:13-14 WEB)

He wrote that everything apart from the Creator (God) is vanity. So in conclusion, the best thing we can do in life is to worship God and keep His commandments - His instructions laid out for us in the Bible. There are commandments under the New Covenant of Grace today but they are not the Ten Commandments of the Law. The commandments under Grace were taught by Jesus: Believe in Jesus, and love one another. That's it! Under Grace, we don't have to fulfil these commandments as a burdensome obligation. When we spend time in God's word and see the goodness that God has given to us, we will naturally believe in Jesus and love others as an overflow of the grace that we have received.

It seems like Solomon was not only wise at earning material riches but also at earning eternal riches. Follow his investment advice which is divinely inspired by God, and you will surely reap bountiful eternal rewards when you stand before Jesus' throne in the future.

Righting the Imbalance in this World

Why does God reward a person? Is it out of His love or is it because of His righteousness? It is actually because of His righteousness, but He also enjoys blessing us with good rewards.

"When they had gone out of the city, and were not yet far off, Joseph said to his steward, "Up, follow after the men. When you overtake them, ask them, 'Why have you rewarded evil for good?" (GENESIS 44:4 WEB)

The verse above is the first mention of the Hebrew word "shalam" in the Bible which means "to reward". It has the idea of repaying someone for their work, to complete, make full and make right.

In the verse, Joseph was hatching a plan to keep his full biological brother Benjamin with him in Egypt by planting incriminating evidence to frame him. The "good" that Joseph did for Benjamin was to host him generously as an honored guest in the palace, while the "evil" was Benjamin's alleged crime of theft. Through the incident, we learn that it is an injustice to reward (or repay) good with evil, and that such injustice demands a punishment to right the imbalance. Only man is capable of injustice. God who is the Righteous Judge cannot do such a thing. He justly rewards good for good and evil for evil.

"Honest balances and scales are Yahweh's; all the weights in the bag are his work. It is an abomination for kings to do wrong, for the throne is established by righteousness." (PROVERBS 16:11-12 WEB)

God rewards a person to right an imbalance in the world. Imagine a set of balance and scales. On one side is a person's good works which carry weight. The more good works a person does, the heavier that side becomes. As a Righteous Judge, God cannot allow unrighteousness to exist in the world without dealing with it. Therefore, He has to balance out the other end of the scale by adding His wages (eternal rewards and earthly blessings) on it.

This is why it's so powerful when you do good works without expecting anything in return from man. Doing so causes an imbalance in the world which God has to fix. If you've not been rewarded by man, then you have to be rewarded by God. If you do good works with the ulterior motive of receiving praises from men, then you'll have no reward from God because the imbalance will already be made right by the praises that you receive. That's why Jesus taught in Matthew 6 to do all your good works in secret! Remember, if there's an imbalance, God has to complete and make it right.

"On that night, the king couldn't sleep. He commanded the book of records of the chronicles to be brought, and they were read to the king. It was found written that Mordecai had told of Bigthana and Teresh, two of the king's eunuchs, who were doorkeepers, who had tried to lay hands on the King Ahasuerus. The king said, "What honor and dignity has been given to Mordecai for this?" Then the king's servants who attended him said, "Nothing has been done for him." The king said, "Who is in the court?" Now Haman had come into the outer court of the king's house, to speak to the king about hanging Mordecai on the gallows that he had prepared for him. The king's servants said to him, "Behold, Haman stands in the court." The king said, "Let him come in." So Haman came in. The king said to him, "What shall be done to the man whom the king delights to honor?" Now Haman said in his heart, "Who would the king delight to honor more than myself?"" (ESTHER 6:1-6 WEB)

Like King Ahasuerus, God also has a type book of records in heaven called a "Book of Memory" (Malachi 3:16-18). Those books contain all the deeds that every human has done throughout history, whether good or bad. If King Ahasuerus, a pagan king, was righteous enough to delight in repaying Mordecai for his good deed, won't God the "King of Kings" be even happier to reward you for all your good works?

"Also to you, Lord, belongs loving kindness, for you reward every man according to his work." (PSALMS 62:12 WEB)

Yes it's very certain that God will reward you for all your good works. Now with all this talk of works, I want to be clear that your salvation (eternal life) is not earned by good works. It can only be received by Grace through believing in Jesus as your Lord and Savior. However, rewarding is different from salvation. Rewards are based on good works whereas salvation is a gift. As a righteous God, God owes you the rewards due to you, if you haven't received any form of repayment for your good works yet.

"Now to him who works, the reward is not counted as grace, but as something owed." (ROMANS 4:4 WEB)

In the verse below, it clearly differentiates in the Hebrew language between the action of rewarding and the reward itself. God rewards you by giving you wages.

"May Yahweh repay your work, and a full reward be given to you from Yahweh, the God of Israel, under whose wings you have come to take refuge."" (RUTH 2:12 WEB)

In the verse above, the word "repay" in Hebrew comes from shalam which is the same meaning as "to reward". It is the action. The word "full" in Hebrew is shalem which has a very close meaning to shalam - to make full, and complete. Lastly, the word "reward" in Hebrew comes from sakar which means wages.

"After these things Yahweh's word came to Abram in a vision, saying, "Don't be afraid, Abram. I am your shield, your exceedingly great reward."" (GENESIS 15:1 WEB)

The word "reward" in the verse above is sakar as well which also means wages. So putting all these truths together: God rewards your good works by giving you wages in order to right the imbalance in the world to make everything full and complete. He is a righteous Rewarder. Hallelujah!

On the other hand, God also rewards evil with evil, also to right an imbalance in the world. If unbelieving evildoers have not received punishment for their wicked deeds, you can be sure that God will (according to His timetable) pour out His wrath upon them and dish out the pain they deserve.

"Repay no one evil for evil. Respect what is honorable in the sight of all men. If it is possible, as much as it is up to you, be at peace with all men. Don't seek revenge yourselves, beloved, but give place to God's wrath. For it is written, "Vengeance belongs to me; I will repay, says the Lord." Therefore "If your enemy is hungry, feed him. If he is thirsty, give him a drink; for in doing so, you will heap coals of fire on his head." Don't be overcome by evil, but overcome evil with good." (ROMANS 12:17-21 WEB)

That's why the Bible says to leave room for God to avenge you. If you repay your enemies with evil, not only are you sinning and disappointing God, but you are disqualifying your enemy from receiving punishment from God Himself. God doesn't want us to be self-righteous vigilantes dealing out our own twisted sense of justice - let the judicial system of each government do it. God said that vengeance is His, so let us not be foolish enough to rob Him of what belongs to Him.

"Let every soul be in subjection to the higher authorities, for there is no authority except from God, and those who exist are ordained by God. Therefore he who resists the authority, withstands the ordinance of God; and those who withstand will receive to themselves judgment. For rulers are not a terror to the good work, but to the evil. Do you desire to have no fear of the authority? Do that which is good, and you will have praise from the same, for he is a servant of God to you for good. But if you do that which is evil, be afraid, for he doesn't bear the sword in vain; for he is a servant of God, an avenger for wrath to him who does evil. Therefore you need to be in subjection, not only because of the wrath, but also for conscience' sake. For this reason you also pay taxes, for they are servants of God's service, attending continually on this very thing. Therefore give everyone what you owe: if you owe taxes, pay taxes; if customs, then customs; if respect, then respect; if honor, then honor." (ROMANS 13:1-7 WEB)

The passage above tells us that every government that has been set up is ordained by God. Yes even those corrupt ones that we read about in the news - kingdoms rise and fall and they are all sovereignly in God's control. For example, God raised up Nebuchadnezzar's powerful kingdom of Babylon to be His servant to deal judgment upon Israel (Jeremiah 25:9). Just as easily as He bestowed glory upon Nebuchadnezzar, He made Nebuchadnezzar insane to humble him and strip him of all the glory which he arrogantly credited to himself (Daniel 4:28-37). Just as simple as it was to cause Babylon to rise in power, He caused it to fall in one night at the hands of the Medes and Persians (Daniel 5).

Therefore let us submit to our government's authority and give them the proper respect, knowing that by obeying, we are submitting to God's sovereignty. Governments are servants of God whether they know it or not, and they act as avengers to execute wrath on evildoers. If they, like Pontius Pilate, fail in their duty to serve justice righteously (Matthew 27:24), don't worry. God will be sure to serve the punishment that slipped through the cracks. Not one sin in this world will be left unpunished before eternity begins. If you have been unjustly treated and the perpetrator did not get punished for it, be encouraged because God has recorded it in a Book of Memory, and He will deal with it on your behalf.

"The Lord said, "Who then is the faithful and wise steward, whom his lord will set over his household, to give them their portion of food at the right times? Blessed is that servant whom his lord will find doing so when he comes. Truly I tell you, that he will set him over all that he has. But if that servant says in his heart, 'My lord delays his coming,' and begins to beat the menservants and the maidservants, and to eat and drink, and to be drunken, then the lord of that servant will come in a day when he isn't expecting him, and in an hour that he doesn't know, and will cut him in two, and place his portion with the unfaithful. That servant, who knew his lord's will, and didn't prepare, nor do what he wanted, will be beaten with many stripes, but he who didn't know, and did things worthy of stripes, will be beaten with few stripes. To whomever much is given, of him will much be required; and to whom much was entrusted, of him more will be asked." (LUKE 12:42-48 WEB)

Based on Jesus' parable on the previous page, I believe that there will be differing levels of pain experienced by those who will be in the lake of fire forever. Those who received a greater revelation of Jesus and yet still rejected Him as their Messiah will suffer more pain than those who only received a small revelation of Jesus. I don't think there will be different sections or levels of the lake of fire with correspondingly different levels of intensity, but the differing factor will be the spirit of each unbeliever. During the Great White Throne Judgment at the end of time, based on the sentence of condemnation that is passed by Jesus, it is possible that each unbeliever's pain-sensitivity will be adjusted to the appropriate level based on the evil works committed as well as the level of revelation of Jesus that he or she rejected. They will all be burning in the same lake of fire, but each unbeliever will be experiencing a uniquely-tuned level of pain.

"Then he will say also to those on the left hand, 'Depart from me, you cursed, into the eternal fire which is prepared for the devil and his angels;" (MATTHEW 25:41 WEB)

If I were to make a guess of who will be experiencing the greatest level of pain, I would say it's Satan. He will not be sipping cocktails while ruling over the lake of fire - His screams of pain will be the loudest! He has been filling up the cup of wrath for himself throughout history and he is still stubbornly increasing the 'pain-meter' with unrepentant wicked deeds. You can sure that he will receive what's coming to him.

"The Jews answered him, "We have a law, and by our law he ought to die, because he made himself the Son of God." When therefore Pilate heard this saying, he was more afraid. He entered into the Praetorium again, and said to Jesus, "Where are you from?" But Jesus gave him no answer. Pilate therefore said to him, "Aren't you speaking to me? Don't you know that I have power to release you, and have power to crucify you?" Jesus answered, "You would have no power at all against me, unless it were given to you from above. Therefore he who delivered me to you has greater sin."" (JOHN 19:7-11 WEB)

In the passage above, Jesus said that the one who delivered Him to Pilate has greater sin - There are differing levels of sin, and therefore as a Righteous Judge, God will serve the proper level of punishment required for each unbeliever. Isn't it so assuring to know that God is the Righteous Judge? He will not withhold any rewards that's due to you, and He will not withhold any punishment that's due to your unbelieving enemies. Life is not unfair. Under God's rulership, you can confidently believe that everyone will get what they righteously deserve!

The Book of Life and the Book of Memory

"I saw a great white throne, and him who sat on it, from whose face the earth and the heaven fled away. There was found no place for them. I saw the dead, the great and the small, standing before the throne, and they opened books. Another book was opened, which is the book of life. The dead were judged out of the things which were written in the books, according to their works. The sea gave up the dead who were in it. Death and Hades gave up the dead who were in them. They were judged, each one according to his works. Death and Hades were thrown into the lake of fire. This is the second death, the lake of fire. If anyone was not found written in the book of life, he was cast into the lake of fire." (REVELATION 20:11-15 WEB)

The passage above teaches us that there are at least two types of books about us that God has in heaven: The Book of Memory which records the deeds of every person, and the Book of Life which records the names of every person who will have eternal life.

Additionally, we learn that the only criteria for someone to be thrown into the lake of fire is that his name is not in the Book of Life. These two types of books are written at different points in time.

Firstly, Books of Memory are written progressively as time passes. It is probably the angels in heaven who record the deeds of men in such books as they happen in real-time, as can be seen from the following passage.

"Then those who feared Yahweh spoke one with another; and Yahweh listened, and heard, and a book of memory was written before him, for those who feared Yahweh, and who honored his name. They shall be mine," says Yahweh of Armies, "my own possession in the day that I make, and I will spare them, as a man spares his own son who serves him. Then you shall return and discern between the righteous and the wicked, between him who serves God and him who doesn't serve him." (MALACHI 3:16-18 WEB)

When the priests spoke words which proved that they feared the Lord, a (not "the" which proves that there is more than one) Book of Memory was written to record their act of faith. For believers, the records in these books will be referred to when it's time to stand before Jesus to receive rewards. For sinners (unbelievers), the Books of Remembrance about them will be referred to so as to determine the severity of their punishment in the lake of fire.

Like a friend recently told me, "God is the best Accountant". He keeps such a meticulous record of man's deeds, both good and evil, so that Jesus will not shortchange anyone on the day of judgment. The righteous will get their due rewards, and the wicked will get their due punishments. Jesus is such a righteous Judge!

The book that David is referring to in the following verse is the Book of Memory about his life.

"You count my wanderings. You put my tears into your container. Aren't they in your book?" (PSALM 56:8 WEB)

In another psalm, David speaks to God about his anger towards wicked people. The Bible records what David wrote accurately, but it doesn't mean that what David wrote is what God will do. God records a person's sins precisely as it should be. He doesn't add extra accountability to it, neither does He mitigate it.

"Charge them with crime upon crime. Don't let them come into your righteousness. Let them be blotted out of the book of life, and not be written with the righteous." (PSALM 69:27-28 WEB)

On top of that, God doesn't blot anyone's name out of the Book of Life. You see, although the Books of Memory are written progressively as time passes, the Book of Life was written and completed since the foundation of the world.

"It was given to him to make war with the saints, and to overcome them. Authority over every tribe, people, language, and nation was given to him. All who dwell on the earth will worship him, everyone whose name has not been written from the foundation of the world in the book of life of the Lamb who has been killed." (REVELATION 13:7-8 WEB)

This means that God doesn't add or remove names from the Book of Life anymore. It is a perfectly-completed book. The passage above says that those whose names are not in the Book of Life will worship the antichrist during the Great Tribulation. It's important to get this truth right: Their names are not in the Book of Life not because they worship the antichrist. They worship the antichrist because their names are not in the Book of Life!

Don't get me wrong, God doesn't create us in His mind one by one and think: "Hmm, I'm going to choose Samantha to be saved so she is going to be in the Book of Life, but I'm creating Sandy to burn in the lake of fire eventually, so I'm not going to add her name in the Book of Life." No, the Book of Life is not written to decide each individual's salvation.

Instead, it is an accurate, objective record of God's foreknowledge of what will happen throughout time. God simply recorded all the names of those who will choose to believe in Him and receive salvation of their own free will.

When God decided to create man with a free will, being omniscient (all-knowing), He could look into the future and know exactly who will chose to believe in Him and who will reject Him, even before these people are even born. Since God can choose what actions He will take throughout the passage of time, He probably chose the total set of actions that would lead to the best outcome: the highest number of people being saved, since He doesn't show favoritism (Acts 10:34). That's why God's word says that we are elected, selected and predestined for salvation from the foundation of the world.

God saw the set of His actions that would lead to the highest number of people being saved, and He said yes to creating man with free will, effectively predestining us for salvation. It is still us choosing to believe in Him of our own free will, but He already knew long ago that we would do so. I know that this is confusing, but when I finally understood it, everything makes sense.

No one is created to burn in the lake of fire. We all choose our own eternal fate of our own free will, but God already knows who will believe in Him and who won't. That's why God's word says that His desire is for all to come to repentance and that no one should perish. But the consequence of free will is that some will believe in Him and some won't. Therefore, since the Book of Life is a completed book, no one's name can be blotted out from it today. This proves that our salvation is eternally secure - once we believe in Jesus, we already have eternal life and will always remain saved.

"He who overcomes will be arrayed in white garments, and I will in no way blot his name out of the book of life, and I will confess his name before my Father, and before his angels." (REVELATION 3:5 WEB)

God talked about the Book of Life through the prophet Ezekiel, and called it by another name, "The Writing of the House of

Israel". This is probably a code name before it was revealed openly in the New Testament as the Book of Life.

"My hand will be against the prophets who see false visions and who utter lying divinations. They will not be in the council of my people, neither will they be written in the writing of the house of Israel, neither will they enter into the land of Israel. Then you will know that I am the Lord Yahweh."" (EZEKIEL 13:9 WEB)

The Book of Life is a writing of names of the house of Israel because all Gentile believers are added into the true and eternal Israel (born of the Spirit and not of the flesh) like wild olive shoots which are grafted into a natural olive tree.

"But if some of the branches were broken off, and you, being a wild olive, were grafted in among them and became partaker with them of the root and of the richness of the olive tree," (ROMANS 11:17 WEB)

So all believers, whether Jew or Gentile, are part of the "House of Israel". Rejoice child of God, for your name is recorded in the Book of Life! On Judgment Day, you can stand confidently before Jesus' throne and know that the only things you're going to receive are rewards and the confirmation of eternal life. With this bold assurance of faith, you can live a victorious life in Christ, full of hope for the future, enjoying freedom from fear and condemnation!

When Secrecy is a Good Thing

You know those business deals whereby the two parties agreeing to the terms and conditions sign a non-disclosure agreement so that it remains confidential? Well you see, if you want to receive heavenly rewards from the activities of charity, praying, fasting, and all other activities that merit rewards, then you have to respect the non-disclosure agreement between God and you.

"Be careful that you don't do your charitable giving before men, to be seen by them, or else you have no reward from your Father who is in heaven. Therefore, when you do merciful deeds, don't sound a trumpet before yourself, as the hypocrites do in the synagogues and in the streets, that they may get glory from men. Most certainly I tell you, they have received their reward. But when you do merciful deeds, don't let your left hand know what your right hand does, so that your merciful deeds may be in secret, then your Father who sees in secret will reward you openly. "When you pray, you shall not be as the hypocrites, for they love to stand and pray in the synagogues and in the corners of the streets, that they may be seen by men. Most certainly, I tell you, they have received their reward. But you, when you pray, enter into your inner room, and having shut your door, pray to your Father who is in secret; and your Father who sees in secret will reward you openly. In praying, don't use vain repetitions as the Gentiles do; for they think that they will be heard for their much speaking. Therefore don't be like them, for your Father knows what things you need before you ask him... "Moreover when you fast, don't be like the hypocrites, with sad faces. For they disfigure their faces that they may be seen by men to be fasting. Most certainly I tell you, they have received their reward. But you, when you fast, anoint your head and wash your face, so that you are not seen by men to be fasting, but by your Father who is in secret; and your Father, who sees in secret, will reward you. "Don't lay up treasures for yourselves on the earth, where moth and rust consume, and where thieves break through and steal; but lay up for yourselves treasures in heaven, where neither moth nor rust consume, and where thieves don't break through and steal; for where your treasure is, there your heart will be also." (MATTHEW 6:1-8, 16-21 WEB)

In the past before I received this revelation, there were times when I was tithing a big amount (at least in my opinion), like more than a thousand dollars, and I would slowly write the details on the back of the envelope, slowly count the money, double check, and slowly slot in the money into the envelope - all this was done at service while there were people around me. It's a very worldly thing to want to show off when you have something good going for you. Little did I know, by acting in this way, I had no reward in heaven waiting for me from my

Heavenly Father. People who do good deeds to be seen by men just want to look 'religious', 'pious', 'spiritual' and 'good' before others. They purposely donate with a trumpet (social media is the modern day 'trumpet') announcing their charitable act, lengthen a prayer while using advanced vocabulary and quoting scripture to impress men, and fast dramatically by making themselves look like they are suffering so much for the Lord.

All this hypocrisy and pretension is an abomination to God - He hates such behavior. So what does God love? He loves it when you donate because it's well-pleasing to Him, out of a cheerful heart, and out of a genuine compassion for the poor. He loves it when you pray because you want Him to hear it, out of a desire to involve Him in your life, and to spend time in fellowship with Him. He loves it when you fast because you want Him to see it, out of a heart that prioritizes God over all worldly pleasures, with a desire to become more sensitive and obedient to His voice. Basically, He wants you to do all these good things for His eyes only, and not to be recognized by men.

So is it okay to write your tithe amount on the envelope for the church's administrative records? Yes it's okay because the principle behind the non-disclosure agreement between God and you is: don't do things for the sake of showing off to men to satisfy your fleshly pride. As long as your heart is sincere about doing these good works for God and not for men, it is okay. Dear brother or sister in Christ, do it God's way - The rewards stored up for you in heaven will be great!

A White Stone and a New Name

"He who has an ear, let him hear what the Spirit says to the assemblies. To him who overcomes, to him I will give of the hidden manna, and I will give him a white stone, and on the stone a new name written, which no one knows but he who receives it." (REVELATION 2:17 WEB)

There is an eternal reward mentioned by Jesus which I initially found rather cute - it's a white stone. I wondered what it meant, until I read up about the context behind it. The word for "stone" in the passage in Greek, is "psēphon". It means a small, worn, smooth stone, like a pebble. In the ancient courts of justice, the accused were condemned by black pebbles and acquitted by white pebbles. This can be seen in the following words of the Apostle Paul, who was recounting his past of persecuting the early church:

"I myself most certainly thought that I ought to do many things contrary to the name of Jesus of Nazareth. I also did this in Jerusalem. I both shut up many of the saints in prisons, having received authority from the chief priests, and when they were put to death I gave my vote against them." (ACTS 26:9-10 WEB)

The words "my vote" is also "psēphon". Paul cast a black pebble to vote for the saints to be condemned to death. Therefore this white stone that Jesus will give to us represents the fact that we are acquitted of all our sins - we have been completely forgiven.

The first passage of this chapter also says that there will be a new name engraved on the stone that only the recipient will know. In the Bible when God gives someone a new name, it represents a change in that person's life and destiny. God gave Abram a new name and established an everlasting covenant of blessing with him.

"Abram fell on his face. God talked with him, saying, "As for me, behold, my covenant is with you. You will be the father of a multitude of nations. Your name will no more be called Abram, but your name will be Abraham; for I have made you the father of a multitude of nations. I will make you exceedingly fruitful, and I will make nations of you. Kings will come out of you. I will establish my covenant between me and you and your offspring after you throughout their generations for an everlasting covenant, to be a God to you and to your offspring after you. I will give to you, and to your offspring after you, the land where you are traveling, all the land of Canaan, for an everlasting possession. I will be their God."" (GENESIS 17:3-8 AMP)

God gave Sarai a new name and declared blessings upon her.

"God said to Abraham, "As for Sarai your wife, you shall not call her name Sarai, but her name shall be Sarah. I will bless her, and moreover I will give you a son by her. Yes, I will bless her, and she will be a mother of nations. Kings of peoples will come from her."" (GENESIS 17:15-16 WEB)

God gave Jacob a new name, and declared good promises to him.

"God said to him, "Your name is Jacob. Your name shall not be Jacob any more, but your name will be Israel." He named him Israel. God said to him, "I am God Almighty. Be fruitful and multiply. A nation and a company of nations will be from you, and kings will come out of your body. The land which I gave to Abraham and Isaac, I will give it to you, and to your offspring after you I will give the land." (GENESIS 35:10-12 WEB)

I believe that the new name that will be engraved on your white stone represents your newfound blessings and special role to God in the eternal city of New Jerusalem on the new earth. He will give you a new name, and it will be your little secret between you and God - a special, exclusive relationship - What an awesome reward!

The Biblical Secret of Ministry Growth

""I know your works, and your toil and perseverance, and that you can't tolerate evil men, and have tested those who call themselves apostles, and they are not, and found them false. You have perseverance and have endured for my name's sake, and have not grown weary. But I have this against you, that you left your first love. Remember therefore from where you have fallen, and repent and do the first works; or else I am coming to you swiftly, and will move your lamp stand out of its place, unless you repent." (REVELATION 2:2-5 WEB)

For this chapter, I would like to begin by defining a "ministry" as a platform that God entrusts a believer with, enabling him/her to serve the Lord. It is like a calling that's actively being fulfilled. Some ministries grow steadily and healthily by God's Grace and favor, while others struggle along to barely stay afloat. What is the reason for this big difference in results? In Revelation 2 and 3, the ascended Lord Jesus commands the apostle John to write to the respective seven churches in Asia, and each church receives a tailor-made letter specifically addressing their situation.

"To the angel of the assembly in Ephesus write: "He who holds the seven stars in his right hand, he who walks among the seven golden lamp stands says these things:" (REVELATION 2:1 WEB)

Notice who each letter is addressed to: the translated word "angel" is "ággelos" in Greek which means either messenger or angel. In this context, I believe that Jesus is speaking to the head pastor of each local church.

To the head pastor of the Ephesians church, Jesus is saying in the passage of the day that He recognizes all the hard work that he is doing for the Lord. However, unknowingly, the pastor is putting himself under the Law instead of relying on God's Grace - toiling and laboring to earn God's approval rather than working from a position of knowing that he is already approved and loved by God.

Being under the Law, that pastor lost that awesome sense of eternal security in his heart that he is completely forgiven and so loved by God. Perhaps the more he learned about the word of God, the more he transitioned into a mode of focusing on what he had to do instead of what Jesus has already done for him. This type of Christianity is a loveless one, sometimes even stressful, tiring and makes a person bitter, angry and unhappy. It is the work of the devil. Most likely, this pastor is teaching these wrong beliefs to his congregation as well, harming their spiritual health.

"You are alienated from Christ, you who desire to be justified by the law. You have fallen away from grace. For we, through the Spirit, by faith wait for the hope of righteousness. For in Christ Jesus neither circumcision amounts to anything, nor uncircumcision, but faith working through love. You were running well! Who interfered with you that you should not obey the truth? This persuasion is not from him who calls you. A little yeast grows through the whole lump. I have confidence toward you in the Lord that you will think no other way. But he who troubles you will bear his judgment, whoever he is." (GALATIANS 5:4-10 WEB)

Whenever we go from being justified entirely by God's Grace, to trying to earn our own justification (to be forgiven and declared righteous) through good works, we have fallen from Grace. That's what the devil tries to do in our lives. He sprinkles a tiny bit of Law-based teaching in our ears and soon the pure grace teachings of the Gospel in our hearts are corrupted. That's why we must be very careful about who we allow to speak into our ears, especially regarding the Gospel. It can make the difference between a victorious, flourishing ministry, or a defeated, struggling one. The Lord Jesus then tells the head pastor of the Ephesian church to: 1) Remember from where he has fallen - Meaning to identify and correct the wrong believing he has, 2) Repent - To replace the wrong belief with a right belief, 3) Do the first works - but what does this mean?

"But woe to you Pharisees! For you tithe mint and rue and every herb, but you bypass justice and God's love. You ought to have done these, and not to have left the other undone." (LUKE 11:42 WEB)

"Woe to you, scribes and Pharisees, hypocrites! For you tithe mint, dill, and cumin, and have left undone the weightier matters of the law: justice, mercy, and faith. But you ought to have done these, and not to have left the other undone." (MATTHEW 23:23 WEB)

In the two verses above, notice that Jesus rebuked the scribes and Pharisees not because they tithed, but because they neglected the more important issues: Justice, God's Love, Mercy and Faith. Therefore, when Jesus told the head pastor of the Ephesian church to do the first works, the word first in Greek is "prótos" which means "most important", not just first in terms of sequential order. What Jesus means is focus on learning about justice, God's love, mercy and faith, and teaching them to the congregation instead of preaching on justification by works and keeping the Law which produces wrong believing, leading to a defeated Christian life. Finally, Jesus said that if the head pastor would not do the above, He would remove the local church (the pastor's ministry), and most likely, He would lead the congregation to sit under another pastor's ministry to receive the right teachings about the Gospel. Jesus our Good Shepherd will always ensure that His flock gets well-fed with the right spiritual food.

When we encounter a ministry that's preaching Law or mixture instead of true Grace, what should we do? Well Jesus did commend the pastor in the passage of the day for testing and exposing the false apostles. From a motivation of love, we can warn other believers about false teachings (if we're sure about it) just like the apostle Paul did, but that shouldn't be the sole focus of our ministry. I read powerful words somewhere that instead of focusing on exposing the darkness, we should just shine the light into the darkness and it will scatter. Sharing about God's Grace should always be our primary focus. I love the wise advice that Gamaliel gave with regards to what to do when encountering a (possibly) heretical ministry - Let's read it.

"But one stood up in the council, a Pharisee named Gamaliel, a teacher of the law, honored by all the people, and commanded to put the apostles out for a little while. He said to them, "You men of Israel, be careful concerning these men, what you are about to do. For before these days Theudas rose up, making himself out to be somebody; to whom a number of men, about four hundred, joined themselves: who was slain; and all, as many as obeyed him, were dispersed, and came to nothing. After this man, Judas of Galilee rose up in the days of the enrollment, and drew away some people after him. He also perished, and all, as many as obeyed him, were scattered abroad. Now I tell you, withdraw from these men, and leave them alone. For if this counsel or this work is of men, it will be overthrown. But if it is of God, you will not be able to overthrow it, and you would be found even to be fighting against God!"" (ACTS 5:34-39 WEB)

What brilliant advice! It is the embodiment of faith and resting in God's power, goodness and righteousness. Gamaliel is saying that if a ministry spreads false teachings, God is the One who will overthrow it. It is not up to us to do it. Just like in the passage of the day, Jesus said that if the head pastor didn't repent He would be the One to remove the ministry from his hands. Whereas if the ministry is actually teaching correctly, operating in the will of God and we are misunderstood about it due to our own lack of revelation, trying to stop it will be like ramming our heads against a brick wall - We will just harm ourselves and not be able to prevent what God is doing.

If we want to see our ministry grow and experience promotion from the Lord, we must conduct our ministry with the truth of God's Grace and accurate teachings of Jesus' death, resurrection and ascension. The title of "apostle" was given to those who were eyewitnesses of Jesus in His resurrected body. What do you think they preached about most of the time? The truth of Jesus', death, resurrection, ascension and what Jesus' finished work has accomplished for us of course!

"They went out, and preached everywhere, the Lord working with them, and confirming the word by the signs that followed. Amen." (MARK 16:20 WEB)

"They continued steadfastly in the apostles' teaching and fellowship, in the breaking of bread, and prayer. Fear came on every soul, and many wonders and signs were done through the apostles. All who believed were together, and had all things in common. They sold their possessions and goods, and distributed them to all, according as anyone had need. Day by day, continuing steadfastly with one accord in the temple, and breaking bread at home, they took their food with gladness and singleness of heart, praising God, and having favor with all the people. The Lord added to the assembly day by day those who were being saved." (ACTS 2:42-47 WEB)

The portions of Scripture above reveals the secret of a ministry's growth to us. When accurate teachings of God's word goes forth from a ministry, the Lord will promote it. Does it mean we shun or avoid the parts of the Bible about the Law, such as Exodus, Leviticus, Deuteronomy, etc?

"But we know that the law is good, if a person uses it lawfully, as knowing this, that law is not made for a righteous person, but for the lawless and insubordinate, for the ungodly and sinners, for the unholy and profane, for murderers of fathers and murderers of mothers, for manslayers, for the sexually immoral, for homosexuals, for slave-traders, for liars, for perjurers, and for any other thing contrary to the sound doctrine; according to the Good News of the glory of the blessed God, which was committed to my trust." (1 TIMOTHY 1:8-11 WEB)

As Paul teaches, we should still teach or share about the Law in it's proper context today: to make unbelievers realize that they are sinful and can't earn forgiveness from God by themselves; so that they will recognize their need for a Savior - Our Lord Jesus. The Law presents the problem, and Grace is the solution. When a ministry uses the Law correctly to exalt God's Grace, it be rewarded on earth by growing and producing powerful results - accompanying signs and wonders as well as numerous salvations. Additionally, as you will learn later on in this book, winning souls for the kingdom of God will help you accumulate great eternal rewards too!

You Won't go Broke from Being Generous

"Jesus sat down opposite the treasury, and saw how the multitude cast money into the treasury. Many who were rich cast in much. A poor widow came, and she cast in two small brass coins, which equal a quadrans coin. He called his disciples to himself, and said to them, "Most certainly I tell you, this poor widow gave more than all those who are giving into the treasury, for they all gave out of their abundance, but she, out of her poverty, gave all that she had to live on." (MARK 12:41-44 WEB)

In the past when I read or heard the passage above being preached, I would always be inspired by the widow's faith & generosity and find that it was a pity that she would stay poor - I assumed that her situation wouldn't change. However I missed out one important truth: Jesus saw her. Whenever Jesus saw someone being generous to Him or His Father in heaven, they would receive a blessing of provision that exceeded what they gave.

Peter and his fellow fishermen caught nothing all night but when Peter lent his boat to Jesus, Jesus compensated him with a miraculous catch of fishes.

"Now while the multitude pressed on him and heard the word of God, he was standing by the lake of Gennesaret. He saw two boats standing by the lake, but the fishermen had gone out of them, and were washing their nets. He entered into one of the boats, which was Simon's, and asked him to put out a little from the land. He sat down and taught the multitudes from the boat. When he had finished speaking, he said to Simon, "Put out into the deep, and let down your nets for a catch." Simon answered him, "Master, we worked all night, and took nothing; but at your word I will let down the net." When they had done this, they caught a great multitude of fish, and their net was breaking. They beckoned to their partners in the other boat, that they should come and help them. They came, and filled both boats, so that they began to sink. But Simon Peter, when he saw it, fell down at Jesus' knees, saying, "Depart from me, for I am a sinful man, Lord." For he was amazed, and all who were with him, at the catch of fish which they had caught; and so also were James and John, sons of Zebedee, who were partners with Simon. Jesus said to Simon, "Don't be afraid. From now on you will be catching people alive." When they had brought their boats to land, they left everything, and followed him." (LUKE 5:1-11 WEB)

Jesus did not say "Hey I am God, you have to give Me your boat because I command you to". Instead, He blessed Peter immediately after, with earthly blessings, and not just heavenly rewards in the future.

"Bring the whole tithe into the storehouse, that there may be food in my house, and test me now in this," says Yahweh of Armies, "if I will not open you the windows of heaven, and pour you out a blessing, that there will not be room enough for." (MALACHI 3:10 WEB)

Under the Law, Israel was commanded to tithe to the Levitical priesthood, but now under Grace, we don't give towards the kingdom of God out of obligation, but out of a heart of thankfulness towards God for blessing us with everything that we have. When Peter gave his boat to Jesus, God literally poured out such a great blessing that there was not enough room on the two boats to receive it! If under the Law the blessings of the tithe were so great, imagine how much more blessed we are today when we give to God under grace.

Did you also notice how the generosity of God towards them did not cause them to become worldly and covet the money they would receive from selling the huge catch of fish? God's goodness led to their repentance - they decided to follow Jesus and count everything else as insignificant in comparison. God's supply of provision also did not just bless Peter, but it filled the other boat with fish too - God blesses us to be a blessing to others as well.

In another incident, we see a little boy generously giving all that he had: two fishes and five barley loaves to share with everyone else.

"After these things, Jesus went away to the other side of the sea of Galilee, which is also called the Sea of Tiberias. A great multitude followed him, because they saw his signs which he did on those who were sick. Jesus went up into the mountain, and he sat there with his disciples. Now the Passover, the feast of the Jews, was at hand. Jesus therefore lifting up his eyes, and seeing that a great multitude was coming to him, said to Philip, "Where are we to buy bread, that these may eat?" He said this to test him, for he himself knew what he would do. Philip answered him, "Two hundred denarii worth of bread is not sufficient for them, that every one of them may receive a little." One of his disciples, Andrew, Simon Peter's brother, said to him, "There is a boy here who has five barley loaves and two fish, but what are these among so many?" Jesus said, "Have the people sit down." Now there was much grass in that place. So the men sat down, in number about five thousand. Jesus took the loaves; and having given thanks, he distributed to the disciples, and the disciples to those who were sitting down; likewise also of the fish as much as they desired. When they were filled, he said to his disciples, "Gather up the broken pieces which are left over, that nothing be lost." So they gathered them up, and filled twelve baskets with broken pieces from the five barley loaves, which were left over by those who had eaten." (JOHN 6:1-13 WEB)

Jesus didn't say to the little boy "Give me your food! Go hungry because it's a good chance to fast and learn some patience." Instead, Jesus blessed him right there with earthly blessings and not just heavenly rewards in the future. Not only was the boy's stomach satisfied, but the multiplication of the food fed 5000 other men too. The boy was blessed to be a blessing to multitudes! Later on, Jesus also instructed His disciples to bless the households that received them with blessings of favor, wellbeing and prosperity.

"Jesus sent these twelve out and commanded them, saying, "Don't go among the Gentiles, and don't enter into any city of the Samaritans. Rather, go to the lost sheep of the house of Israel. As you go, preach, saying, 'The Kingdom of Heaven is at hand!' Heal the sick, cleanse the lepers, and cast out demons. Freely you received, so freely give. Don't take any gold, silver, or brass in your money belts. Take no bag for your journey, neither two coats, nor sandals, nor staff: for the laborer is worthy of his food. Into whatever city or village you enter, find out who in it is worthy, and stay there until you go on. As you enter into the household, greet it. If the household is worthy, let your peace come on it, but if it isn't worthy, let your peace return to you." (MATTHEW 10:5-13 WEB)

Their generosity towards God's messengers resulted in both earthly and heavenly blessings to them. God is a God who rewards generosity with generosity.

"He who receives you receives me, and he who receives me receives him who sent me. He who receives a prophet in the name of a prophet will receive a prophet's reward. He who receives a righteous man in the name of a righteous man will receive a righteous man's reward. Whoever gives one of these little ones just a cup of cold water to drink in the name of a disciple, most certainly I tell you, he will in no way lose his reward." (MATTHEW 10:40-42 WEB)

Every act of generosity that we do results in a reward from God. When the Philippian church sponsored the Apostle Paul's ministry, not only did they receive profits to their heavenly account, they also received the assurance from Paul that God would liberally supply their every need on earth according to the riches in glory in Christ Jesus.

"However you did well that you shared in my affliction. You yourselves also know, you Philippians, that in the beginning of the Good News, when I departed from Macedonia, no assembly shared with me in the matter of giving and receiving but you only. For even in Thessalonica you sent once and again to my need. Not that I seek for the gift, but I seek for the fruit that increases to your account. But I have all things and abound. I am filled, having received from Epaphroditus the things that came from you, a sweet-smelling fragrance, an acceptable and well-pleasing sacrifice to God. My God will supply every need of yours according to his riches in glory in Christ Jesus." (PHILIPPIANS 4:14-19 WEB)

When they gave, they were not short-changed - God gave them both earthly and heavenly blessings as a reward for their generosity.

The following is probably my favorite passage of Scripture about giving and receiving.

"I thought it necessary therefore to entreat the brothers that they would go before to you and arrange ahead of time the generous gift that you promised before, that the same might be ready as a matter of generosity, and not of greediness.

Remember this: he who sows sparingly will also reap sparingly. He who sows bountifully will also reap bountifully. Let each man give according as he has determined in his heart, not grudgingly or under compulsion, for God loves a cheerful giver. And God is able to make all grace abound to you, that you, always having all sufficiency in everything, may abound to every good work. As it is written, "He has scattered abroad. He has given to the poor. His righteousness remains forever." Now may he who supplies seed to the sower and bread for food, supply and multiply your seed for sowing, and increase the fruits of your righteousness, you being enriched in everything to all generosity, which produces thanksgiving to God through us. For this service of giving that you perform not only makes up for lack among the saints, but abounds also through much giving of thanks to God, seeing that through the proof given by this service, they glorify God for the obedience of your confession to the Good News of Christ and for the generosity of your contribution to them and to all, while they themselves also, with supplication on your behalf, yearn for you by reason of the exceeding grace of God in you. Now thanks be to God for his unspeakable gift!" (2 CORINTHIANS 9:5-15 WEB)

Here are the lessons about giving and receiving from the passage above: We reap financial blessings according to the measure in which we sow. We should give cheerfully, the amount in which we are happy to give in our heart, which is led by the Holy Spirit. Believers are enriched by God so that we can do good works, charity and be generous. Our acts of generosity indirectly produces thanksgivings to God. We receive prayers from the beneficiaries of our financial gift. Our giving supplies the need of the saints.

We shouldn't give reluctantly or grudgingly because it is a sin to do that. Yes even if you give a large amount like US$1,000,000 unwillingly, it's still sinning.

"But he who doubts is condemned if he eats, because it isn't of faith; and whatever is not of faith is sin." (ROMANS 14:23 WEB)

In the first passage of this chapter we read about the rich people who were putting large amounts of money into the temple treasury. We don't know whether they were giving reluctantly or not, and we don't know the motive behind their giving. After all, they gave out of their surplus, whereas the poor widow gave everything that she had. Before giving, always examine the state of your heart - are you happy to give this amount? Good if the answer is yes. If not, perhaps reduce the amount to what you are comfortable with - be a cheerful giver. Who will God bless more? The stingy believer or the generous believer? The generous one of course!

"There is one who scatters, and increases yet more. There is one who withholds more than is appropriate, but gains poverty. The liberal soul shall be made fat. He who waters shall be watered also himself. People curse someone who withholds grain, but blessing will be on the head of him who sells it." (PROVERBS 11:24-26 WEB)

God wants to bless others through you - the blessing is supposed to flow through you, not just stop at you. If someone else is willing to be obedient to allow God's blessings to reach those whom He intends to reach, won't He bless that obedient believer more instead? The selfish believer won't starve, but he or she probably won't be entrusted with great riches like the generous believer. Remember that we are enriched so that we can be generous. Someone who is stingy to others and only generous to himself will find that he will become poor.

"He who loves pleasure will be a poor man. He who loves wine and oil won't be rich." (PROVERBS 21:17 WEB)

Is this a punishment for selfishness? No it is allowed to happen to lead a believer back to God. Just like how the prodigal son was allowed to lose everything when he wasted his entire inheritance on sinful pursuits.

"He said, "A certain man had two sons. The younger of them said to his father, 'Father, give me my share of your property.' So he divided his livelihood between them. Not many days after, the younger son gathered all of this together and traveled into a far country. There he wasted his property with riotous living. When he had spent all of it, there arose a severe famine in that country, and he began to be in need. He went and joined himself to one of the citizens of that country, and he sent him into his fields to feed pigs. He wanted to fill his belly with the husks that the pigs ate, but no one gave him any. But when he came to himself he said, 'How many hired servants of my father's have bread enough to spare, and I'm dying with hunger! I will get up and go to my father, and will tell him, "Father, I have sinned against heaven, and in your sight. I am no more worthy to be called your son. Make me as one of your hired servants."' "He arose, and came to his father. But while he was still far off, his father saw him, and was moved with compassion, and ran, and fell on his neck, and kissed him. The son said to him, 'Father, I have sinned against heaven and in your sight. I am no longer worthy to be called your son.' "But the father said to his servants, 'Bring out the best robe, and put it on him. Put a ring on his hand, and sandals on his feet. Bring the fattened calf, kill it, and let's eat, and celebrate; for this, my son, was dead, and is alive again. He was lost, and is found.' Then they began to celebrate." (LUKE 15:11-24 WEB)

After the son learnt his lesson, he was restored and was well-provided for. God's heart is for us to enjoy His abundance, but He values the growth of our character more than our material comfort. If there is a lesson to be taught, He won't hesitate to let us be uncomfortable for a season, until we learn the lesson.

So back to our main story. Did the widow who gave the two copper coins go broke from being generous? I don't think she did. Maybe she had no money for a short while, but God definitely blessed her with provision, just like how He blessed the widow in the following story through the prophet Elisha (who represents Jesus).

"Now a certain woman of the wives of the sons of the prophets cried out to Elisha, saying, "Your servant my husband is dead. You know that your servant feared Yahweh. Now the creditor has come to take for himself my two children to be slaves." Elisha said to her, "What should I do for you? Tell me: what do you have in the house?" She said, "Your servant has nothing in the house, except a pot of oil." Then he said, "Go, borrow empty containers from all your neighbors. Don't borrow just a few containers. Go in and shut the door on you and on your sons, and pour oil into all those containers; and set aside those which are full." So she went from him, and shut the door on herself and on her sons. They brought the containers to her, and she poured oil. When the containers were full, she said to her son, "Bring me another container." He said to her, "There isn't another container." Then the oil stopped flowing. Then she came and told the man of God. He said, "Go, sell the oil, and pay your debt; and you and your sons live on the rest." (2 KINGS 4:1-7 WEB)

You see, the widow probably thought that no one saw her put everything that she had into the temple treasury. But guess what? Jesus was watching, just like how God in heaven keeps an account of every secret act of generosity that we do. You can be sure that He sees every gift that you have given with a cheerful and sincere heart, and you will receive both earthly and heavenly blessings as a result. Therefore like Jesus says, stop being worried.

"Therefore I tell you, don't be anxious for your life: what you will eat, or what you will drink; nor yet for your body, what you will wear. Isn't life more than food, and the body more than clothing? See the birds of the sky, that they don't sow, neither do they reap, nor gather into barns. Your heavenly Father feeds them. Aren't you of much more value than they? "Which of you by being anxious, can add one moment‡ to his lifespan? Why are you anxious about clothing? Consider the lilies of the field, how they grow. They don't toil, neither do they spin, yet I tell you that even Solomon in all his glory was not dressed like one of these. But if God so clothes the grass of the field, which today exists and tomorrow is thrown into the oven, won't he much more clothe you, you of little faith? "Therefore don't be anxious, saying, 'What will we eat?', 'What will we drink?' or, 'With what will we be clothed?' For the Gentiles seek after all these things; for your heavenly Father knows that you need all these things. But seek first God's Kingdom and his righteousness; and all these things will be given to you as well. Therefore don't be anxious for tomorrow, for tomorrow will be anxious for itself. Each day's own evil is sufficient." (MATTHEW 6:25-34 WEB)

Open up your heart and wallet - feel free to be generous. You will not go broke, and you will not starve. The One who owns the cattle on a thousand hills is your financial backer!

"For every animal of the forest is mine, and the livestock on a thousand hills. I know all the birds of the mountains. The wild animals of the field are mine. If I were hungry, I would not tell you, for the world is mine, and all that is in it." (PSALM 50:10-12 WEB)

He will continue to pour out the resources from heaven's treasury on you so that you can keep doing generous, charitable deeds which are adding both earthly and heavenly rewards to your account. Hallelujah!

The Rewards of Persecution and Martyrdom

God promised in His word that all believers who desire to live a godly life devoted to Him will face persecution.

"Yes, and all who desire to live godly in Christ Jesus will suffer persecution." (2 TIMOTHY 3:12 WEB)

The Book of Daniel tells two stories of believers having faith in God that leads to their deliverance from harm. One of them is "Daniel in the Lion's Den", and the other which we will be focusing on in this chapter, is the story of "Shedrach, Meshach and Abed-Neto rescued from the Burning Furnace".

"Nebuchadnezzar the king made an image of gold, whose height was sixty cubits, and its width six cubits. He set it up in the plain of Dura, in the province of Babylon. Then Nebuchadnezzar the king sent to gather together the local governors, the deputies, and the governors, the judges, the treasurers, the counselors, the sheriffs, and all the rulers of the provinces, to come to the dedication of the image which

Nebuchadnezzar the king had set up. Then the local governors, the deputies, and the governors, the judges, the treasurers, the counselors, the sheriffs, and all the rulers of the provinces, were gathered together to the dedication of the image that Nebuchadnezzar the king had set up; and they stood before the image that Nebuchadnezzar had set up. Then the herald cried aloud, "To you it is commanded, peoples, nations, and languages, that whenever you hear the sound of the horn, flute, zither, lyre, harp, pipe, and all kinds of music, you fall down and worship the golden image that Nebuchadnezzar the king has set up. Whoever doesn't fall down and worship shall be cast into the middle of a burning fiery furnace the same hour." (DANIEL 3:1-6 WEB)

Notice that the height of the golden statue is 60 cubits, and the width and length of it are 6 cubits by 6 cubits? That's 666 - The number of the beast who is the antichrist to come during the Great Tribulation - the time of the greatest persecution against Christians. The clue of 666 will allow Christians who are alive during the antichrist's lifetime to figure out who he is.

"He deceives my own people who dwell on the earth because of the signs he was granted to do in front of the beast, saying to those who dwell on the earth that they should make an image to the beast who had the sword wound and lived. It was given to him to give breath to it, to the image of the beast, that the image of the beast should both speak, and cause as many as wouldn't worship the image of the beast to be killed. He causes all, the small and the great, the rich and the poor, and the free and the slave, to be given marks on their right hands, or on their foreheads; and that no one would be able to buy or to sell, unless he has that mark, which is the name of the beast or the number of his name. Here is wisdom. He who has understanding, let him calculate the number of the beast, for it is the number of a man. His number is six hundred sixty-six." (REVELATION 13:14-18 AMP)

We who are believers now will not go through the Great Tribulation because it will only begin after Jesus takes us away to be with Him during the Rapture. The word "rebellion" in the passage below is the Greek word "apostasia" which is translated as "departure" and "departing away" in some other Bible versions. I believe that it is referring to the Rapture.

"Let no one deceive you in any way. For it will not be, unless the rebellion comes first, and the man of sin is revealed, the son of destruction, he who opposes and exalts himself against all that is called God or that is worshiped, so that he sits as God in the temple of God, setting himself up as God. Don't you remember that, when I was still with you, I told you these things? Now you know what is restraining him, to the end that he may be revealed in his own season. For the mystery of lawlessness already works. Only there is one who restrains now, until he is taken out of the way. Then the lawless one will be revealed, whom the Lord will kill with the breath of his mouth, and destroy by the manifestation of his coming; even he whose coming is according to the working of Satan with all power and signs and lying wonders, and with all deception of wickedness for those who are being lost, because they didn't receive the love of the truth, that they might be saved." (2 THESSALONIANS 2:3-10 WEB)

I believe that the devil is already scheming how he can mislead the most number of souls as he can during the coming Great Tribulation. As the passage above says, he will have the permission to deceive the world with "all deception of wickedness" during that time. The only thing preventing that dreadful event from happening right now is the Holy Spirit Who is indwelling every believer. The Holy Spirit is the One who is restraining this evil. Once we are taken away during the Rapture, the Holy Spirit's presence will no longer be on earth, and the Great Tribulation will begin. However people who will believe in Jesus after the Rapture have to go through the Great Tribulation and they will definitely face persecution from the antichrist.

The measurements of Nebuchadnezzar's golden statue tells us that this story in the Book of Daniel is pointing to a similar persecution that post-Rapture believers will face during the Great Tribulation.

"Now if you are ready whenever you hear the sound of the horn, flute, zither, lyre, harp, pipe, and all kinds of music to fall down and worship the image which I have made, good; but if you don't worship, you shall be cast the same hour into the middle of a burning fiery furnace. Who is that god who will deliver you out of my hands?" Shadrach, Meshach, and Abednego answered the king, "Nebuchadnezzar, we have no need to answer you in this matter. If it happens, our God whom we serve is able to deliver us from the burning fiery furnace; and he will deliver us out of your hand, O king. But if not, let it be known to you, O king, that we will not serve your gods or worship the golden image which you have set up." (DANIEL 3:15-18 WEB)

Just like what will happen during the Great Tribulation, King Nebuchadnezzar (an antichrist figure) commanded that whoever did not worship the image would be put to death - in this case, death by burning in the furnace. He was forcing everyone to commit the sin of idolatry - worshipping anything other than the one true God. Take a look at the courageous response of Shadrach, Meshach and Abed-nego. They refused to betray their faith in the true God. They trusted that God was on their side and that God was more powerful than whatever King Nebuchadnezzar could do to them. The three men were also prepared to die for their faith in God as well. I can only say that they are shining examples of believers who have complete faith in God.

King Nebuchadnezzar was furious when he heard their response and he commanded for the three men to be thrown into the burning furnace. Let's see what happened next.

"Then Nebuchadnezzar the king was astonished and rose up in haste. He spoke and said to his counselors, "Didn't we cast three men bound into the middle of the fire?" They answered the king, "True, O king." He answered, "Look, I see four men loose, walking in the middle of the fire, and they are unharmed. The appearance of the fourth is like a son of the gods." Then Nebuchadnezzar came near to the mouth of the burning fiery furnace. He spoke and said, "Shadrach, Meshach, and Abednego, you servants of the Most High God, come out, and come here!" Then Shadrach, Meshach, and Abednego came out of the middle of the fire. The local governors, the deputies, and the governors, and the king's counselors, being gathered together, saw these men, that the fire had no power on their bodies. The hair of their head wasn't singed. Their pants weren't changed, the smell of fire wasn't even on them." (DANIEL 3:24-27 WEB)

Despite the heavy persecution that Shadrach, Meshach and Abed-nego faced, they were able to persevere in faith and God sent a divine figure whom I believe is the Pre-Incarnate Christ to rescue them from death. It was a perfect deliverance - they were not injured at all. The passage above describes the fourth man as "a son of the gods" which would certainly seem that way to King Nebuchadnezzar who had pagan beliefs which embraced the idea of multiple gods (a polytheistic religion).

I believe that God had a divine purpose for this miraculous and dramatic rescue of the three men. It could be for the sake of testifying to King Nebuchadnezzar and everyone present that the Lord is the true God. Something good came out of this persecution: the Lord was honored and received glory through it.

"Nebuchadnezzar spoke and said, "Blessed be the God of Shadrach, Meshach, and Abednego, who has sent his angel and delivered his servants who trusted in him, and have changed the king's word, and have yielded their bodies, that they might not serve nor worship any god, except their own God. Therefore I make a decree, that every people, nation, and language, which speak anything evil against the God of Shadrach, Meshach, and Abednego, shall be cut in pieces, and their houses shall be made a dunghill; because there is no other god who is able to deliver like this." (DANIEL 3:28-29 WEB)

Such a decree from the king would possibly stir up the curiosity and faith of the people of Babylon, giving them the opportunity to believe in the true God instead of worshipping false idols.

God doesn't rescue believers from death through persecution all the time. Stephen was the first martyr of the church. He was persecuted for his faith in Jesus and stoned to death. He was a faithful believer, yet God deemed fit that he should die at that time. Sometimes, by God's divine purposes, believers become martyrs (believers who die because of persecution) for their faith. We hear and read of stories like that, especially in countries where there is strong persecution against Christians. We must pray for these brave Christians to have the faith to endure through the persecutions. But we can be encouraged and rejoice for them because they will receive great eternal rewards.

"I know your works and where you dwell, where Satan's throne is. You hold firmly to my name, and didn't deny my faith in the days of Antipas my witness, my faithful one, who was killed among you, where Satan dwells." (Revelation 2:13 WEB)

Jesus sees and will not forget the sacrifice that the martyrs make. Essentially, martyrs are doing what Jesus did at the cross for us: they are obedient to God even to the point of death - and that holds great rewards because it is the ultimate sign of their unwavering faith in God. On the other hand, for the believers who go through persecution and do not become martyrs in the process, they can be encouraged too, for they will also receive great rewards and restoration for their faith. The 'Hall of Faith' in Hebrews 11 records how Moses endured persecution in Egypt because of his faith in God and that there is a great reward for him to look forward to.

"By faith, Moses, when he had grown up, refused to be called the son of Pharaoh's daughter, choosing rather to share ill treatment with God's people than to enjoy the pleasures of sin for a time, considering the reproach of Christ greater riches than the treasures of Egypt; for he looked to the reward." (HEBREWS 11:24-26 WEB)

As a result of standing firm in their beliefs, Shadrach, Meshach and Abed-nego prospered after facing the persecution! That was their earthly reward and restoration, but there are also additional heavenly rewards stored up for them.

"Then the king promoted Shadrach, Meshach, and Abednego in the province of Babylon." (DANIEL 3:30 WEB)

What the three men experienced reminds me of a passage in Psalm 66.

" For you, God, have tested us. You have refined us, as silver is refined. You brought us into prison. You laid a burden on our backs. You allowed men to ride over our heads. We went through fire and through water, but you brought us to the place of abundance." (Psalm 66:10-12 WEB)

Sometimes, very sadly, persecution can even come from a believer's own family.

"Peter began to tell him, "Behold, we have left all, and have followed you." Jesus said, "Most certainly I tell you, there is no one who has left house, or brothers, or sisters, or father, or mother, or wife, or children, or land, for my sake, and for the sake of the Good News, but he will receive one hundred times more now in this time: houses, brothers, sisters, mothers, children, and land, with persecutions; and in the age to come eternal life." (Mark 10:28-30 WEB)

However, we shouldn't despair because Jesus Himself promised that such believers who choose to hold on to their faith even if it means sacrificing familial relationships, will receive a hundredfold worth of rewards in this life and more rewards for eternity as well. God is a good God who rewards us when we place our faith in Him. Notice that Jesus said "with persecutions" too which means that there will always be persecution as long as you live a life that is devoted to Jesus. That's because the devil hates it when Christians do that, and will stop at nothing to try to destroy Christians who live by faith. The devil has no problem with a believer who lives like a sinner, but when a believer lives like a redeemed child of God, the devil comes roaring angrily like a lion, trying to devour him or her.

"Blessed be the God and Father of our Lord Jesus Christ, the Father of mercies and God of all comfort; who comforts us in all our affliction, that we may be able to comfort those who are in any affliction, through the comfort with which we ourselves are comforted by God. For as the sufferings of Christ abound to us, even so our comfort also abounds through Christ." (II Corinthians 1:3-5 WEB)

If you've lost anything or anyone dear to you because of persecution, God will give you the strength to continue on in life. He is the "God of all comfort, who comforts us in all our affliction". To wrap up this chapter, I'm going to share a secret of divine protection in the story of Shadrach, Meshach and Abed-nego for Christians who go through persecution. This revelation came to me when I studied the meaning of the names of these three men.

"Now among these were of the children of Judah: Daniel, Hananiah, Mishael, and Azariah. The prince of the eunuchs gave names to them: to Daniel he gave the name Belteshazzar; to Hananiah, Shadrach; to Mishael, Meshach; and to Azariah, Abednego." (DANIEL 1:6-7 WEB)

You see, Shadrach's original Hebrew name was Hananiah which means "Yahweh is Gracious". Meshach's original Hebrew name was Mishael which means "Who is Equal to Yahweh?". Abed-Nego's original Hebrew name was Azariah which means "Yahweh has Helped". Yahweh is one of the names of God which many Christians believe to refer to Jesus. When you rely on Jesus' grace and see Him as a good God who loves you even in the midst of persecution, that's the first step to walking in His divine protection. Secondly, realize that your problems are small compared to Jesus, and He is simply greater than anything else. Focus on how powerful He is instead of focusing on how heavy the persecution is. Lastly, always meditate on the times where Jesus has helped you or delivered you out of a trial. If He has done so before, He will do it again - believe in His everlasting goodness and love for you. When you have this right believing, it places you in the best spiritual state to receive God's divine protection for your life, even in the midst of heavy persecution.

"I have told you these things, that in me you may have peace. In the world you have trouble; but cheer up! I have overcome the world." (JOHN 16:33 WEB)

I don't know what persecution you are facing, but I know that Jesus has promised that we can enjoy His perfect peace and joy even in the midst of persecution. We can do so because through the cross, Jesus has already overcome the world and conquered Satan, sin and death!

Be Rewarded for Overcoming Evil with Good

"A fool shows his annoyance the same day, but one who overlooks an insult is prudent." (PROVERBS 12:16 WEB)

Do you remember the last time you were insulted? Do you remember the feelings of anger and indignation rising up within you (or is it just me)? God's word says that a prudent person ignores an insult. In fact, Jesus is the Master at ignoring insults. Let's take a look at how He did it while on earth. After being arrested by Caiaphas the High Priest, Jesus was interrogated by the religious leaders of Israel so that they might find evidence to put Him to death by.

"Now the chief priests, the elders, and the whole council sought false testimony against Jesus, that they might put him to death, and they found none. Even though many false witnesses came forward, they found none. But at last two false witnesses came forward and said, "This man said, 'I am able to destroy the temple of God, and to build it in three days.'" The high priest stood up and said to him, "Have you no answer? What is this that these testify against you?" But Jesus stayed silent. The high priest answered him, "I adjure you by the living God that you tell us whether you are the Christ, the Son of God." Jesus said to him, "You have said so. Nevertheless, I tell you, after this you will see the Son of Man sitting at the right hand of Power, and coming on the clouds of the sky." Then the high priest tore his clothing, saying, "He has spoken blasphemy! Why do we need any more witnesses? Behold, now you have heard his blasphemy. What do you think?" They answered, "He is worthy of death!" (MATTHEW 26:59-66 WEB)

The same incident is recorded in the gospel of Mark.

"Now the chief priests and the whole council sought witnesses against Jesus to put him to death, and found none. For many gave false testimony against him, and their testimony didn't agree with each other. Some stood up, and gave false testimony against him, saying, "We heard him say, 'I will destroy this temple that is made with hands, and in three days I will build another made without hands.' " Even so, their testimony didn't agree. The high priest stood up in the middle, and asked Jesus, "Have you no answer? What is it which these testify against you?" But he stayed quiet, and answered nothing. Again the high priest asked him, "Are you the Christ, the Son of the Blessed?" Jesus said, "I am. You will see the Son of Man sitting at the right hand of Power, and coming with the clouds of the sky." The high priest tore his clothes, and said, "What further need have we of witnesses? You have heard the blasphemy! What do you think?" They all condemned him to be worthy of death." (MARK 14:55-64 WEB)

Did you notice that Jesus doesn't respond to those who say "You're not God". He reveals Himself to those who ask Him, "Are You God?", even if they have evil intentions. Again Jesus did the same thing when He was brought before Pontius Pilate.

"Now Jesus stood before the governor; and the governor asked him, saying, "Are you the King of the Jews?" Jesus said to him, "So you say." When he was accused by the chief priests and elders, he answered nothing. Then Pilate said to him, "Don't you hear how many things they testify against you?" He gave him no answer, not even one word, so that the governor marveled greatly." (MATTHEW 27:11-14 WEB)

Jesus did not respond to any accusations, but He responded when Pilate asked Him "Are You the King of the Jews?". To those who are closed-minded, who have given up trying to understand and who have already passed the verdict of condemnation in their hearts, Jesus ignores. To those who are asking questions (a sign of seeking to understand), He answers. Dear brother or sister in Christ, there is no point in defending, explaining or justifying yourself when the other person has already set in his/her heart to condemn you no matter what. You'll just end up angry, frustrated and even looking desperate. It's foolishness. You don't have to be the last one to get a word in.

As long as your conscience before God is clear, that's all that matters. God will prove it on your behalf in due time if you're really innocent. Don't give weight to the words of your unreasonable critics - haters are going to hate anyway no matter what you do. Jesus showed us at the cross who we should be talking to when facing insults and false accusations.

"Then there were two robbers crucified with him, one on his right hand and one on the left. Those who passed by blasphemed him, wagging their heads and saying, "You who destroy the temple and build it in three days, save yourself! If you are the Son of God, come down from the cross!" Likewise the chief priests also mocking with the scribes, the Pharisees, and the elders, said, "He saved others, but he can't save himself. If he is the King of Israel, let him come down from the cross now, and we will believe in him. He trusts in God. Let God deliver him now, if he wants him; for he said, 'I am the Son of God.'" The robbers also who were crucified with him cast on him the same reproach. Now from the sixth hour there was darkness over all the land until the ninth hour. About the ninth hour Jesus cried with a loud voice, saying, "Eli, Eli, lima sabachthani?" That is, "My God, my God, why have you forsaken me?" (MATTHEW 27:38-46 WEB)

While suspended on the cross, Jesus did not respond to the nasty insults of the people around Him. The only person He responded to was God His Father. This was the worst moment in Jesus' life on earth. He who has always enjoyed unbroken fellowship with God temporarily lost that closeness with God when all the sins of the world were laid upon Him. Losing the favor of God at that moment was far more devastating than the stripes on His body, the nails in His limbs, or the struggle of lifting the entire weight of His body up to breathe. The suffering He was going through did not cause Him to lash out in anger at the people around who were pouring out poisonous insults. He did not command legions of angels to descend and kill the wicked people who were mocking Him. I declare to you that God is your Vindicator. He will give you the justice that's due to you - you don't have to become a vigilante and try to serve up your own self-righteous form of justice.

"Bless those who persecute you; bless, and don't curse. Rejoice with those who rejoice. Weep with those who weep. Be of the same mind one toward another. Don't set your mind on high things, but associate with the humble. Don't be wise in your own conceits. Repay no one evil for evil. Respect what is honorable in the sight of all men. If it is possible, as much as it is up to you, be at peace with all men. Don't seek revenge yourselves, beloved, but give place to God's wrath. For it is written, "Vengeance belongs to me; I will repay, says the Lord." Therefore "If your enemy is hungry, feed him. If he is thirsty, give him a drink; for in doing so, you will heap coals of fire on his head." Don't be overcome by evil, but overcome evil with good." (ROMANS 12:14-21 WEB)

If you cannot ignore and must say or do something to those who persecute you with insults and false accusations, then do this: Bless them, pray for them, in front of them if possible. Be extremely nice to them and even become the nicest person in their life. By doing so, you're heaping burning coals (of guilt) on their heads. In this way, you overcome evil with good, and possibly make a friend out of an enemy. Recognize that the devil and his demons are behind this, influencing the person to dislike, insult and falsely accuse you. Your true enemy is the invisible evil spirit, not the person who is insulting you.

"For our wrestling is not against flesh and blood, but against the principalities, against the powers, against the world's rulers of the darkness of this age, and against the spiritual forces of wickedness in the heavenly places." (EPHESIANS 6:12 WEB)

The devil wants you to react with evil so that he has both you and that person under his power. But if you start making a friend every time he sends someone to insult you, maybe he'll think twice about continuing to do that. The answer is never to fight fire with fire, but to extinguish the fire with the water of God's grace.

"No weapon that is formed against you will prevail; and you will condemn every tongue that rises against you in judgment. This is the heritage of Yahweh's servants, and their righteousness is of me," says Yahweh. No weapon that is formed against you will succeed; And every tongue that rises against you in judgment you will condemn. This [peace, righteousness, security, and triumph over opposition] is the heritage of the servants of the LORD, And this is their vindication from Me," says the LORD." (ISAIAH 54:17 WEB)

Weapons will be formed and tongues will rise up in judgment, but the good news is: they will not prevail against you. Ignore the insults and overcome evil with good! And the cherry on top? You get rewarded with both earthly and heavenly rewards - the passage below doesn't quantify what type of rewards so feel free to claim both in Jesus' name.

"If your enemy is hungry, give him food to eat. If he is thirsty, give him water to drink; for you will heap coals of fire on his head, and Yahweh will reward you." (PROVERBS 25:21-22 WEB)

Praise the Lord for His goodness which is exceedingly and abundantly above what we can think or imagine!

Same Throne, Different Judgments

"But you, why do you judge your brother? Or you again, why do you despise your brother? For we will all stand before the judgment seat of Christ. For it is written, " 'As I live,' says the Lord, 'to me every knee will bow. Every tongue will confess to God.' " So then each one of us will give account of himself to God." (Romans 14:10-12 WEB)

It is clear from the passage above that the context is that everyone will stand before the judgment seat of Christ - Aside from "we shall all stand", the Apostle Paul also quotes the Lord's words "every knee shall bow to Me, and every tongue shall confess to God".

The word "judgment" is actually translated from the Greek word "bema" which means a raised place mounted by steps, like a platform, rostrum or tribunal. Two other examples of bema seat in the Bible are the seat on a raised platform where Pilate sat in to speak to the public and the throne on a raised platform that Herod deliver speeches to the people from. So it doesn't actually mean that everyone who stands before Jesus' bema seat will be under judgment in a scary "punishment" sort of way. In the future both believers and unbelievers will stand before Jesus' throne (I know it's a throne because of the Great White Throne that the Apostle John saw and wrote about in the Book of Revelation), but at different times and for different purposes.

"Therefore also we make it our aim, whether at home or absent, to be well pleasing to him. For we must all be revealed before the judgment seat of Christ that each one may receive the things in the body according to what he has done, whether good or bad. Knowing therefore the fear of the Lord, we persuade men, but we are revealed to God, and I hope that we are revealed also in your consciences." (II Corinthians 5:9-11 WEB)

Firstly, believers will not be judged (punished) by Jesus for the wrongdoings they have committed in their lifetime. Jesus already paid for all our sins at the cross so God cannot punish us for them again. Believers will stand before Jesus' throne, before the Great White Throne Judgment takes place, to receive rewards for the good works that they have done in their lifetime, like acts of faith and service to the Lord.

"Behold, I come quickly. My reward is with me, to repay to each man according to his work." (REVELATION 22:12 WEB)

On the other hand, unbelievers will stand before Jesus' throne to receive their sentence of eternal torment in the lake of fire. No one is sinless. The moment we were born, we already had sin coursing through our blood which we inherited from our parents. The unbelievers will try to use the good works that they have done as a basis for forgiveness, but it won't work - all of them have fallen short of the glory of God. No one can be justified by his own works - if they could do that, Jesus wouldn't have needed to die for us.

Some of Jesus' parables shed light on how He will reward believers and condemn unbelievers in the future. Firstly, let's examine Jesus' Parable of the Minas.

"As they heard these things, he went on and told a parable, because he was near Jerusalem, and they supposed that God's Kingdom would be revealed immediately. He said therefore, "A certain nobleman went into a far country to receive for himself a kingdom and to return. He called ten servants of his and gave them ten mina coins, and told them, 'Conduct business until I come.' But his citizens hated him, and sent an envoy after him, saying, 'We don't want this man to reign over us.' "When he had come back again, having received the kingdom, he commanded these servants, to whom he had given the money, to be called to him, that he might know what they had gained by conducting business. The first came before him, saying, 'Lord, your mina has made ten more minas.' "He said to him, 'Well done, you good servant! Because you were found faithful with very little, you shall have authority over ten cities.' "The second came, saying, 'Your mina, Lord, has made five minas.' "So he said to him, 'And you are to be over five cities.' Another came, saying, 'Lord, behold, your mina, which I kept laid away in a handkerchief, for I feared you, because you are an exacting man. You take up that which you didn't lay down, and reap that which you didn't sow.' "He said to him, 'Out of your own mouth I will judge you, you wicked servant! You knew that I am an exacting man, taking up that which I didn't lay down, and reaping that which I didn't sow. Then why didn't you deposit my money in the bank, and at my coming, I might have earned interest on it?' He said to those who stood by, 'Take the mina away from him and give it to him who has the ten minas.' "They said to him, 'Lord, he has ten minas!' 'For I tell you that to everyone who has, will more be given; but from him who doesn't have, even that which he has will be taken away from him. But bring those enemies of mine who didn't want me to reign over them here, and kill them before me.' " (LUKE 19:11-27 WEB)

The three servants who gave account to the king represent believers, the king represents Jesus, and the enemies killed by the king represent unbelievers. In the parable, we see that the greatness of the rewards depends on how faithful a believer is in using his gifts to fulfil his calling from God during his lifetime. Those who are the wisest at using their gifts for the Lord will receive greater rewards than the good works that they have done. Conversely, those believers who neglect their gifts because of wrong believing like that third servant will have eternal life, but not receive much rewards on top of that. Unbelievers will not have any rewards at all - they will be sentenced to the "second death" - never-ending suffering in the lake of fire.

Next, let's look at Jesus' Parable of the Talents.

"For it is like a man going into another country, who called his own servants and entrusted his goods to them. To one he gave five talents, to another two, to another one, to each according to his own ability. Then he went on his journey. Immediately he

69

who received the five talents went and traded with them, and made another five talents. In the same way, he also who got the two gained another two. But he who received the one talent went away and dug in the earth and hid his lord's money. "Now after a long time the lord of those servants came, and settled accounts with them. He who received the five talents came and brought another five talents, saying, 'Lord, you delivered to me five talents. Behold, I have gained another five talents in addition to them.' "His lord said to him, 'Well done, good and faithful servant. You have been faithful over a few things, I will set you over many things. Enter into the joy of your lord.' "He also who got the two talents came and said, 'Lord, you delivered to me two talents. Behold, I have gained another two talents in addition to them.' "His lord said to him, 'Well done, good and faithful servant. You have been faithful over a few things. I will set you over many things. Enter into the joy of your lord.' "He also who had received the one talent came and said, 'Lord, I knew you that you are a hard man, reaping where you didn't sow, and gathering where you didn't scatter. I was afraid, and went away and hid your talent in the earth. Behold, you have what is yours.' "But his lord answered him, 'You wicked and slothful servant. You knew that I reap where I didn't sow, and gather where I didn't scatter. You ought therefore to have deposited my money with the bankers, and at my coming I should have received back my own with interest. Take away therefore the talent from him and give it to him who has the ten talents. For to everyone who has will be given, and he will have abundance, but from him who doesn't have, even that which he has will be taken away. Throw out the unprofitable servant into the outer darkness, where there will be weeping and gnashing of teeth.' " (MATTHEW 25:14-30 WEB)

The parable above is very similar to the Parable of the Minas but there are different characters in this one. The first two servants represent believers, the third servant represents an unbeliever and the master represents Jesus. This parable reveals something new to us which is that Jesus (through the Holy Spirit) gives different measures of gifts to everyone by His sovereign choice. He doesn't expect us to produce more fruits than the gifts that we have received from Him. It can be clearly seen by this: although the first servant produced five more talents and the second servant only produced two more talents, they both received the same praise from the master: "Well done, good and faithful servant. You have been faithful over a few things, I will set you over many things. Enter into the joy of your lord.".

If Jesus anointed you with the gift of writing, then write for Him! He won't expect you to become a world-class praise and worship leader. He will provide for what He creates. Although we believers now won't be judged by Jesus before His throne during the "Great White Throne Judgment", there will be future generation of believers who will stand before His throne to be declared righteous. Those generations of believers are the ones who will believe in Jesus during the Millennial Reign of Christ. They will be raised from the dead together with all the unbelievers and stand before Jesus' throne at the end of the Millennial Reign of Christ. The believers will be acquitted, receive rewards and go into eternal life while the unbelievers will be condemned to the lake of fire.

"I saw a great white throne, and him who sat on it, from whose face the earth and the heaven fled away. There was found no place for them. I saw the dead, the great and the small, standing before the throne, and they opened books. Another book was opened, which is the book of life. The dead were judged out of the things which were written in the books, according to their works. The sea gave up the dead who were in it. Death and Hades gave up the dead who were in them. They were judged, each one according to his works. Death and Hades were thrown into the lake of fire. This is the second death, the lake of fire. If anyone was not found written in the book of life, he was cast into the lake of fire." (REVELATION 20:11-15 WEB)

Recorded in the books are all the deeds that everyone has done in their lifetime, whether good or bad. The believers will be judged by their works there to determine their eternal rewards, and they will have eternal life because their names are written in the Book of Life. On the other hand, the unbelievers whose names are not recorded in the Book of Life will try to merit their salvation through the good works that they did during their lifetime, but it won't be enough. Their works will condemn them, not acquit them.

Unbelieving Jews will be judged according to the Law, whereas unbelieving Gentiles will be judged according to their conscience. No amount of charity or volunteer work can earn a person total forgiveness of sins. The only way a person can be saved today is to believe in Jesus Christ.

"For as many as have sinned without the law will also perish without the law. As many as have sinned under the law will be judged by the law. For it isn't the hearers of the law who are righteous before God, but the doers of the law will be justified (for when Gentiles who don't have the law do by nature the things of the law, these, not having the law, are a law to themselves, in that they show the work of the law written in their hearts, their conscience testifying with them, and their thoughts among themselves accusing or else excusing them) in the day when God will judge the secrets of men, according to my Good News, by Jesus Christ." (ROMANS 2:12-16 WEB)

Notice that there are three parties that give up their dead during the Judgment? The sea, death and Hades (hell). The sea represents the Gentile nations - those Gentiles who will die when the whole earth is burned up by divine fire, before the judgment takes place. This will be elaborated on in the next chapter. In the Bible, sometimes the "sea" is used as a symbol to represent the Gentile nations. In Daniel's prophecy below, the sea represents the Gentile nations. All four empires that he saw were Gentile nations - Babylonian, Medo-Persian, Greek and Roman.

"Daniel spoke and said, "I saw in my vision by night, and, behold, the four winds of the sky broke out on the great sea. Four great animals came up from the sea, different from one another. "The first was like a lion, and had eagle's wings. I watched until its wings were plucked, and it was lifted up from the earth, and made to stand on two feet as a man. A man's heart was given to it. "Behold, there was another animal, a second, like a bear. It was raised up on one side, and three ribs were in its mouth between its teeth. They said this to it: 'Arise! Devour much flesh!' "After this I saw, and behold, another, like a leopard, which had on its back four wings of a bird. The animal also had four heads; and dominion was given to it. "After this I saw in the night visions, and, behold, there was a fourth animal, awesome and powerful, and exceedingly strong. It had great iron teeth. It devoured and broke in pieces, and stamped the residue with its feet. It was different from all the animals that were before it. It had ten horns." (DANIEL 7:2-7 WEB)

In the Book of Revelation, the beast emerging from the sea represents the antichrist coming from a Gentile nation.

"Then I stood on the sand of the sea. I saw a beast coming up out of the sea, having ten horns and seven heads. On his horns were ten crowns, and on his heads, blasphemous names." (REVELATION 13:1 WEB)

The dead who are surrendered by Death are the people who will become believers during the Millennial Reign of Christ. They will be dead, but not in hell. I believe they will be waiting in heaven for the Great White Throne Judgment where they will get resurrected to eternal life. The dead given up by Hades (hell) are the unbelievers - both Jews and Gentiles - who had died in their sins without ever placing their faith in God (before Jesus came) or Jesus. They will be suffering in hell until the Great White Throne Judgment.

During the Millennial Reign of Christ, all Israel will become believers, as Paul prophesied.

"They also, if they don't continue in their unbelief, will be grafted in, for God is able to graft them in again. For if you were cut out of that which is by nature a wild olive tree, and were grafted contrary to nature into a good olive tree, how much more will these, which are the natural branches, be grafted into their own olive tree? For I don't desire you to be ignorant, brothers, of this mystery, so that you won't be wise in your own conceits, that a partial hardening has happened to Israel, until the fullness of the Gentiles has come in, and so all Israel will be saved. Even as it is written, There will come out of Zion the Deliverer, and he will turn away ungodliness from Jacob. This is my covenant with them, when I will take away their sins." (ROMANS 11:23-27 WEB)

It is at Second Coming of Christ that the fullness of the Gentiles will have come in. How do I know?

"They will fall by the edge of the sword, and will be led captive into all the nations. Jerusalem will be trampled down by the Gentiles, until the times of the Gentiles are fulfilled. There will be signs in the sun, moon, and stars; and on the earth anxiety of nations, in perplexity for the roaring of the sea and the waves; men fainting for fear, and for expectation of the things which are coming on the world: for the powers of the heavens will be shaken. Then they will see the Son of Man coming in a cloud with power and great glory. But when these things begin to happen, look up and lift up your heads, because your redemption is near." (LUKE 21:24-28 WEB)

Jesus mentioned in the passage above that Jerusalem will be tramped down by the Gentiles until the "times of the Gentiles" are fulfilled. Then He goes on to describe His Second Coming. After the Second Coming of Christ, Jesus will rule from Jerusalem and Jerusalem will become the world's center of power, effective transferring the dominance from the Gentiles to the Jews. During that time which is the Millennial Reign of Christ, God will end the hardening of the natural descendants of Israel's hearts, and lead all of them to believe in Jesus as their Messiah. In this way, that whole generation of Israel will be saved.

Let's go back to our main topic, the judgments. Jesus' Parable of the Sheep and Goats is about the Great White Throne Judgment.

""But when the Son of Man comes in his glory, and all the holy angels with him, then he will sit on the throne of his glory. Before him all the nations will be gathered, and he will separate them one from another, as a shepherd separates the sheep from the goats. He will set the sheep on his right hand, but the goats on the left. Then the King will tell those on his right hand, 'Come, blessed of my Father, inherit the Kingdom prepared for you from the foundation of the world; for I was hungry and you gave me food to eat. I was thirsty and you gave me drink. I was a stranger and you took me in. I was naked and you clothed me. I was sick and you visited me. I was in prison and you came to me.' "Then the righteous will answer him, saying, 'Lord, when did we see you hungry and feed you, or thirsty and give you a drink? When did we see you as a stranger and take you in, or naked and clothe you? When did we see you sick or in prison and come to you?' "The King will answer them, 'Most certainly I tell you, because you did it to one of the least of these my brothers, you did it to me.' Then he will say also to those on the left hand, 'Depart from me, you cursed, into the eternal fire which is prepared for the devil and his angels; for I was hungry, and you didn't give me food to eat; I was thirsty, and you gave me no drink; I was a stranger, and you didn't take me in; naked, and you didn't clothe me; sick, and in prison, and you didn't visit me.' "Then they will also answer, saying, 'Lord, when did we see you hungry, or thirsty, or a stranger, or naked, or sick, or in prison, and didn't help you?' "Then he will answer them, saying, 'Most certainly I tell you, because you didn't do it to one of the least of these, you didn't do it to me.' These will go away into eternal punishment, but the righteous into eternal life." (MATTHEW 25:31-46 WEB)

The sheep in the parable represent the people who become believers during the Millennial Reign of Christ. They will go into eternal life. The goats represent all the unbelievers who exist throughout history. They will all be thrown into the lake of fire for unending punishment. Jesus also described the Great White Throne Judgment when rebuked the Pharisees.

"Either make the tree good and its fruit good, or make the tree corrupt and its fruit corrupt; for the tree is known by its fruit. You offspring of vipers, how can you, being evil, speak good things? For out of the abundance of the heart, the mouth speaks. The good man out of his good treasure brings out good things, and the evil man out of his evil treasure brings out evil things. I tell you that every idle word that men speak, they will give account of it in the day of judgment. For by your words you will be justified, and by your words you will be condemned." (MATTHEW 12:33-37 WEB)

It is clear that Jesus is talking about two different groups when He compares good trees and bad trees, the good man and evil man. So believers will be justified by their words of believing in

Jesus, whereas unbelievers will be condemned because their spoken words prove that they rejected Jesus. So in summary, all believers until the Millennial Reign of Christ will not be judged at the Great White Throne Judgment. They will stand before Jesus' throne before that to receive rewards. However, everyone who becomes a believer during the Millennial Reign of Christ will be at the Great White Throne Judgment to receive rewards and go into eternal life. Finally, all unbelievers will be at the Great White Throne Judgment to receive the sentence of condemnation and be thrown into the lake of fire to be punished forever.

While you're still alive, the most profitable thing you can do from now until the last day of your life on earth, is to accumulate heavenly, eternal rewards to your account. Only those will last forever! I want to end off this chapter with a heavenly tip which reveals another activity that accumulates great eternal rewards.

"The fruit of the righteous is a tree of life. He who is wise wins souls. Behold, the righteous shall be repaid in the earth, how much more the wicked and the sinner!" (PROVERBS 11:30-31 WEB)

Soul-winning is an activity that merits great eternal rewards. Pray for the Lord to lead you how you can share the gospel in the way that He has called you to do it. When one sinner repents, the whole of heaven rejoices! Did you also notice that the passage above says that both the righteous and the wicked will be repaid in the earth? The judgments before the throne of Christ will happen on earth, not in heaven! Let's read more about that in the next chapter.

Fireproof Works Earn us Imperishable Rewards

I want to share about the process by which our eternal rewards will be measured and determined for us. Before we stand in front of Jesus' throne to receive rewards, Jesus will first utterly defeat the devil and his wicked human armies at Jerusalem.

"And after the thousand years, Satan will be released from his prison, and he will come out to deceive the nations which are in the four corners of the earth, Gog and Magog, to gather them together to the war; the number of whom is as the sand of the sea. They went up over the width of the earth, and surrounded the camp of the saints, and the beloved city. Fire came down out of heaven from God and devoured them. The devil who deceived them was thrown into the lake of fire and sulfur, where the beast and the false prophet are also. They will be tormented day and night forever and ever. I saw a great white throne, and him who sat on it, from whose face the earth and the heaven fled away. There was found no place for them." (REVELATION 20:7-11 WEB)

The event above is also prophesied in the Psalms and the Prophets.

"A fire goes before him, and burns up his adversaries on every side. His lightning lights up the world. The earth sees, and trembles. The mountains melt like wax at the presence of Yahweh, at the presence of the Lord of the whole earth." (PSALM 97:3-5 WEB)

Notice that fire and the mountains melting like wax are mentioned again below.

"Hear, you peoples, all of you. Listen, O earth, and all that is therein: and let the Lord Yahweh be witness against you, the Lord from his holy temple. For, behold, Yahweh comes out of his place, and will come down and tread on the high places of the earth. The mountains melt under him, and the valleys split apart, like wax before the fire, like waters that are poured down a steep place." (MICAH 1:2-4 WEB)

I believe this fire that comes down from heaven is not a natural fire which can be resisted by fire-retardant materials. This fire is a divine flame that burns up whatever is temporal, such that even mountains will be melted easily by the fire as if they were wax. According to the passage below, it seems like this fire will not just burn up the area around Jerusalem, but the both the heavens (the sky) and the whole earth as well.

"But the heavens that exist now and the earth, by the same word have been stored up for fire, being reserved against the day of judgment and destruction of ungodly men. But don't forget this one thing, beloved, that one day is with the Lord as a thousand years, and a thousand years as one day. The Lord is not slow concerning his promise, as some count slowness; but he is patient with us, not wishing that anyone should perish, but that all should come to repentance. But the day of the Lord will come as a thief in the night; in which the heavens will pass away with a great noise, and the elements will be dissolved with fervent heat, and the earth and the works that are in it will be burned up. Therefore since all these things will be destroyed like this, what kind of people ought you to be in holy living and godliness, looking for and earnestly desiring the coming of the day of God, which will cause the burning heavens to be dissolved, and the elements will melt with fervent heat? But, according to his promise, we look for new heavens and a new earth, in which righteousness dwells." (2 PETER 3:7-13 WEB) I believe that on the whole earth, only Jerusalem will be safe from the divine fire. The believers will be living in Jerusalem at that time, and they will be uninjured by the flames. Besides, it wouldn't make sense if God burned up Jerusalem too since He sent down fire from heaven in response to Satan and his armies coming against Jerusalem. I'm so glad that God will not slay the believers together with the unbelievers.

"Abraham came near, and said, "Will you consume the righteous with the wicked? What if there are fifty righteous within the city? Will you consume and not spare the place for the fifty righteous who are in it? May it be far from you to do things like that, to kill the righteous with the wicked, so that the righteous should be like the wicked. May that be far from you. Shouldn't the Judge of all the earth do right?" (GENESIS 18:23-25 WEB)

Before God sent the flood, He made sure that Noah, his family and all the animals were safely in the ark first.

"Noah went into the ship with his sons, his wife, and his sons' wives, because of the floodwaters. Clean animals, unclean animals, birds, and everything that creeps on the ground went by pairs to Noah into the ship, male and female, as God commanded Noah. After the seven days, the floodwaters came on the earth." (GENESIS 7:7-10 WEB)

Before God rained fire down from heaven upon Sodom and Gomorrah, He made sure that Lot successfully escaped to Zoar first.

"Hurry, escape there, for I can't do anything until you get there." Therefore the name of the city was called Zoar. The sun had risen on the earth when Lot came to Zoar. Then Yahweh rained on Sodom and on Gomorrah sulfur and fire from Yahweh out of the sky. He overthrew those cities, all the plain, all the inhabitants of the cities, and that which grew on the ground." (GENESIS 19:22-25 WEB)

When God struck Egypt with the plagues, His judgments fell upon the Egyptians but not upon the children of Israel.

"But against any of the children of Israel a dog won't even bark or move its tongue, against man or animal, that you may know that Yahweh makes a distinction between the Egyptians and Israel." (EXODUS 11:7 WEB)

Our Lord judges righteously and makes a clear distinction - He is the Righteous Judge. Hallelujah! After the current earth and heavens are burnt up, there will be a new earth and new heavens, but they will appear only after the dead believers and unbelievers stand before Jesus' throne to receive rewards and condemnation respectively.

"I saw a new heaven and a new earth: for the first heaven and the first earth have passed away, and the sea is no more." (REVELATION 21:1 WEB)

So if all the material elements will be burnt up, then what will remain? The answer is: everything that is eternal.

"whose voice shook the earth then, but now he has promised, saying, "Yet once more I will shake not only the earth, but also the heavens." This phrase, "Yet once more" signifies the removing of those things that are shaken, as of things that have been made, that those things which are not shaken may remain. Therefore, receiving a Kingdom that can't be shaken, let's have grace, through which we serve God acceptably, with reverence and awe, for our God is a consuming fire." (HEBREWS 12:26-29 WEB)

This could explain how the unbelievers can be thrown into the lake of fire during the Great White Throne Judgment because the temporal earth will be gone, exposing the eternal realm that houses the lake of fire. Jerusalem (which will be undamaged by the divine fire) could very possibly be the venue of the Great White Throne Judgment, with the lake of fire burning below it.

"The sea gave up the dead who were in it. Death and Hades gave up the dead who were in them. They were judged, each one according to his works. Death and Hades were thrown into the lake of fire. This is the second death, the lake of fire. If anyone was not found written in the book of life, he was cast into the lake of fire." (REVELATION 20:13-15 WEB)

All our good works done in faith and service to the Lord like helping others, prayer, fasting, charity, enduring persecution and martyrdom will endure the test of divine fire and merit us eternal rewards which cannot be destroyed or lost. How do I know that these works are eternal? Because they have no visible proof of their benefits and have to be done by faith. If God didn't exist, helping others is just wasting your own time, praying is just talking to yourself, fasting is just starving yourself, charity is just robbing your family of resources, enduring persecution and martyrdom is just suffering and dying for a lie.

"to an incorruptible and undefiled inheritance that doesn't fade away, reserved in Heaven for you, who by the power of God are guarded through faith for a salvation ready to be revealed in the last time. Wherein you greatly rejoice, though now for a little while, if need be, you have been grieved in various trials, that the proof of your faith, which is more precious than gold that perishes even though it is tested by fire, may be found to result in praise, glory, and honor at the revelation of Jesus Christ—" (1 PETER 1:4-7 WEB)

Jesus (the Judge on the throne) revealed the secret to us already - it is better to store up rewards in heaven which last forever than treasures on earth which will not stand the test of time or fire.

"Don't lay up treasures for yourselves on the earth, where moth and rust consume, and where thieves break through and steal but lay up for yourselves treasures in heaven, where neither moth nor rust consume, and where thieves don't break through and steal; for where your treasure is, there your heart will be also. "The lamp of the body is the eye. If therefore your eye is sound, your whole body will be full of light. But if your eye is evil, your whole body will be full of darkness. If therefore the light that is in you is darkness, how great is the darkness! "No one can serve two masters, for either he will hate the one and love the other, or else he will be devoted to one and despise the other. You can't serve both God and Mammon." (MATTHEW 6:19-24 WEB)

Choose to serve God - keep your eyes on Him. For in doing so, you will be happier as your hopes will be on God and not on man - Those who rely on man will be disappointed but those who hope in the Lord will never be put to shame. Moreover, when you serve God, you will accumulate both earthly and heavenly blessings to your account. It's obviously the better choice!

"And whatever you do, work heartily, as for the Lord, and not for men, knowing that from the Lord you will receive the reward of the inheritance; for you serve the Lord Christ." (COLOSSIANS 3:23-24 WEB)

Remember Jesus' Parable of the Minas that I wrote about in a previous chapter? The third servant who did not do anything with the mina he received had it taken away from him and didn't receive any rewards. This third servant represents those believers that Paul wrote about in the following passage.

"Now he who plants and he who waters are the same, but each will receive his own reward according to his own labor. For we are God's fellow workers. You are God's farming, God's building. According to the grace of God which was given to me, as a wise master builder I laid a foundation, and another builds on it. But let each man be careful how he builds on it. For no one can lay any other foundation than that which has been laid, which is Jesus Christ. But if anyone builds on the foundation with gold, silver, costly stones, wood, hay, or stubble, each man's work will be revealed. For the Day will declare it, because it is revealed in fire; and the fire itself will test what sort of work each man's work is. If any man's work remains which he built on it, he will receive a reward. If any man's work is burned, he will suffer loss, but he himself will be saved, but as through fire." (1 CORINTHIANS 3:8-15 WEB)

They will have eternal life, but not have any eternal rewards on top of that because they built their lives on worldly, temporal pursuits and foundations which will not survive the test of fire. Many people in the world are so busy climbing the 'success ladder' – don't wait till you're standing at the top and realize that it leads nowhere. How sad it is to labor your entire life and realize that almost everything you did was futile and meaningless. The great news is that we who are alive can still choose to live the rest of our lives focusing on God rather than on anything else that's worldly.

My wife and I once attended a Hillsong worship concert in Singapore at the Star Performing Arts Theatre. We purchased almost front row tickets and had such an amazing and immersive worship experience. We could see the musicians faces clearly. However, imagine if we were standing on the third floor, right at the back by the entrance doors. Wouldn't that drastically decrease the enjoyment of our experience? Similarly, your level of your eternal rewards will make a huge difference in your enjoyment of eternity. You only have one lifetime to earn your 'front row concert ticket'. You can still choose to redeem your time and live wisely to heap up rewards for eternity!

In order to maximize your opportunity to accumulate eternal rewards, there are two main factors: your lifespan, and your good works (the frequency, magnitude, etc.). True believers who have received Jesus as their Lord and Savior that are driven to the point of ending their own lives prematurely won't go to hell or the lake of fire. The Apostle John mentioned suicide in one of his epistles and called it "a sin that leads to death".

"If anyone sees his brother sinning a sin not leading to death, he shall ask, and God will give him life for those who sin not leading to death. There is a sin leading to death. I don't say that he should make a request concerning this." (1 JOHN 5:16 WEB)

But there is one very costly consequence of committing suicide: they lose out on the opportunity to accumulate more eternal rewards. They could have spent eternity with more rewards but they robbed themselves of the blessing. If you feel depressed or suicidal, don't take your life because God has great blessings and rewards in store for you but the devil is trying to steal all that away from you. If he's trying so hard, you know for sure that he can tell that your rewards will be huge! Don't give him the satisfaction or victory. Instead, pray for a long life so that you have more time to accumulate eternal rewards - purposely do the opposite of what the devil wants you to do and he will flee from you because he will realize that his actions are counterproductive to his plans. Psalm 91 promises believers that God will satisfy us with long life, so choose and believe for the number of years that will satisfy you.

" I will satisfy him with long life, and show him my salvation." (PSALM 91:16 WEB)

Burning up the Domain of the 'Aliens'

In the previous chapter, we read that God will send divine fire to burn up both the heavens (the sky) as well as the earth. I understand why He would burn up the earth: as judgment because of the wickedness of man and to defeat the devil and his armies surrounding Jerusalem. However why would God burn up the heavens too? What is wrong with it? The answer has got to do with 'aliens' in the sky. Most people have heard about aliens and these weird creatures are accepted as part of popular culture nowadays. Even kids books, movies and cartoons portray them as beings from outer space that we can become friends with. One popular fictional alien is "ET" which I always found creepy ever since I was a child. If we believers knew the truth about aliens and who they really are, we wouldn't be exposing them to our kids and letting them think it's okay.

"For our wrestling is not against flesh and blood, but against the principalities, against the powers, against the world's rulers of the darkness of this age, and against the spiritual forces of wickedness in the heavenly places." (EPHESIANS 6:12 WEB)

In the verse above, we see a hierarchy of demons: possibly principalities being the highest and spiritual hosts of wickedness being the lowest. Notice that they are in the "heavenly places"? This doesn't mean that they are in heaven (the divine realm). In fact, demons have no access to heaven today.

"She gave birth to a son, a male child, who is to rule all the nations with a rod of iron. Her child was caught up to God, and to his throne… There was war in the sky. Michael and his angels made war on the dragon. The dragon and his angels made war. They didn't prevail. No place was found for them any more in heaven. The great dragon was thrown down, the old serpent, he who is called the devil and Satan, the deceiver of the whole world. He was thrown down to the earth, and his angels were thrown down with him. I heard a loud voice in heaven, saying, "Now the salvation, the power, and the Kingdom of our God, and the authority of his Christ has come; for the accuser of our brothers has been thrown down, who accuses them before our God day and night." (REVELATION 12:5, 7-10 WEB)

The timeline of the passage above happening is after Jesus' death, resurrection and ascension. The male Child being caught up to God represents Jesus' ascension. The devil used to have access to a place in heaven because Adam's rulership rights of the earth were given to Satan. We see in the Book of Job that Satan appeared before God in heaven and that was because as the new federal head of the earth, he had access to Adam's spot.

"Now on the day when God's sons came to present themselves before Yahweh, Satan also came among them. Yahweh said to

Satan, "Where have you come from?" Then Satan answered Yahweh, and said, "From going back and forth in the earth, and from walking up and down in it." (JOB 1:6-7 WEB)

By dying on the cross, Jesus had already righteously paid for the sins of the world and had redeemed the whole earth back from Satan. Satan and his demons tried to protest and fight to maintain Satan's position in heaven but he was permanently evicted and thrown down. So now that we have established that demons have no access to heaven today, then what does the passage of the day mean by "heavenly places"? In the Greek, "heavenly places" is "epouraniois". Besides meaning heaven, it can also refer to the sky where the sun, moon and stars are. We see this in the following passage where the word "heavenly" (in other translations it says "celestial") in Greek is also epouraniois and is used to describe the sun, moon and stars.

"There are also celestial bodies and terrestrial bodies; but the glory of the celestial differs from that of the terrestrial. There is one glory of the sun, another glory of the moon, and another glory of the stars; for one star differs from another star in glory." (1 CORINTHIANS 15:40-41 WEB)

Again in the passage below we see the demons written to be in epouraniois - "heavenly places".

"and to make all men see what is the administration of the mystery which for ages has been hidden in God, who created all things through Jesus Christ, to the intent that now through the assembly the manifold wisdom of God might be made known to the principalities and the powers in the heavenly places, according to the eternal purpose which he accomplished in Christ Jesus our Lord. In him we have boldness and access in confidence through our faith in him." (EPHESIANS 3:9-12 WEB)

When the Apostle Paul wrote this, it was already after Satan and his demons had been permanently cast out of heaven, so they don't have access there anymore. So I believe that today demons only have access to both earth's surface and the "heavenly places": the sky where the sun, moon and stars are. So those strange apparitions in the night skies, unknown flying object (UFO) and alien sightings are probably real. But they aren't aliens, and they aren't friendly. It is demonic activity. No one knows exactly what evil works the demons are doing up there in the sky, but most likely, it is twisted, corrupted and that is why God will burn it up and replace it with new heavens - incinerating the rubbish and starting afresh.

Biblical Ways to Know your Calling in Life

I believe that somewhere along your walk with the Lord, one question you'll have is "What is my calling/purpose in life?". God's word teaches us that there are ways to find out.

1) A strong and lasting desire towards an area of service to the Lord without burning out.

"For it is God who works in you both to will and to work, for his good pleasure." (PHILIPPIANS 2:13 WEB)

Personally, I love reading God's word, seeing the 'hidden Jesus' in the text and writing about the revelations I receive from it. This is something that I enjoy doing and find fulfillment in. It doesn't drain me of energy but it refuels and refreshes me! God provides both the desire and the ability to do it. What do you find yourself constantly drawn back to? Even if you have not done it for a long time but that thing has always been in your heart, like nagging you to get started again. That could very well be a key to knowing your calling in life.

2) Having exceptional talent in a particular skill or area of service.

"Working together, we entreat also that you do not receive the grace of God in vain," (2 CORINTHIANS 6:1 WEB)

There are many different things we can do in life - so many skills and activities that no one can try everything and no one can be good at everything. However one thing I know is that God has blessed you to be good at something and He will lead you on a journey to discover it. You see, it's possible to receive God's grace in vain if you don't use the grace you've been given. When you discover that area or skill in which you have received grace, you will find that you're good at it restfully and easily. Have you discovered which skill you're talented at? If not, pray for God to open your eyes to the gifts that He has already placed inside you. If you're humble, you will be able to discern that it's God's grace working in you and not your own strength.

3) Confirmation from others.

"If any man speaks in another language, let it be two, or at the most three, and in turn; and let one interpret. But if there is no interpreter, let him keep silent in the assembly, and let him speak to himself, and to God. Let the prophets speak, two or three, and let the others discern." (1 CORINTHIANS 14:27-29 WEB)

Although the passage above is talking about the context of speaking in tongues and prophesying, it applies to identifying our calling in life too. Do people tell you that you're good at something, and you find that it's a repeated theme of your life?

At times God will use people to speak prophetically into your life to give you clues. This Christian life isn't meant to be just between you and God only. We are part of the collective body of Christ and each part is interdependent on the whole. We are to help each other to grow in our gifting and ministry for the Lord.

4) Strong resistance and persecution sent by the devil.

"But we, brothers, being bereaved of you for a short season, in presence, not in heart, tried even harder to see your face with great desire, because we wanted to come to you—indeed, I, Paul, once and again—but Satan hindered us. For what is our hope, or joy, or crown of rejoicing? Isn't it even you, before our Lord Jesus at his coming? For you are our glory and our joy." (1 THESSALONIANS 2:17-20 WEB)

It is a pattern in the Bible where the devil tries to stop whatever God is doing. He sees God's activity and tries to sabotage it, but praise the Lord, he always fails in the end. Do you find that often when you're doing something that you love and feel led to, there are sudden, seemingly-random bad things happening all at once? That's the devil trying to hinder something good that God is doing through you. If that happens often enough when you're doing the same type of activity, then the devil is actually indirectly pointing you to God's calling for your life! That's one way that God can turn what is meant for evil to become a tool for good. It is not recorded in the Bible that the Apostle Paul faced any sort of persecution while he was an anti-Jesus Pharisee persecuting the early church. There was no need for the devil to persecute him because he was doing the devil's will. However, when Saul became Paul and started planting churches around the world, he started facing severe persecution that was incited by the devil. This shows clearly that Paul was living out the God-given calling on his life.

5) Evidence of good fruit.

"Even so, every good tree produces good fruit, but the corrupt tree produces evil fruit. A good tree can't produce evil fruit, neither can a corrupt tree produce good fruit." (MATTHEW 7:17-18 WEB)

Which brings me to my next point. Paul's ministry obviously bore much good fruit. The evidence is that the churches he planted were growing - souls were being added to God's kingdom and the new believers were growing in the grace of God. What are you doing that is producing a positive impact on the lives of others? Maybe it's as simple as people becoming happier and encouraged after you do a certain thing? The fruitfulness in something you do can also help in identifying your calling in life.

6) Open doors for an area of service.

"A man's heart plans his course, but Yahweh directs his steps." (PROVERBS 16:9 WEB)

If God has placed a calling on your life, He will surely give you opportunities to fulfill your calling and to grow in that area of gifting. You can't possibly be called to do something if the chance to do that thing never comes up. If you find that the

Lord is repeatedly leading you to do the same type of activity then it could be God revealing your calling in life.

7) Aligned with God's word.

One thing is for sure: Your calling in life will never contradict God's word because His word is His revealed will. God won't call you to become the greatest thief or the most seductive prostitute in the world because stealing and sexual immorality are both sins.

If something you do is aligned with God's word and fulfills the criteria in most of the other points in this chapter, then that thing qualifies to be a potential calling in your life.

You can't know for sure, unless God speaks clearly and directly to you about it, but you can certainly make a wise guess based on all the ways I've shared in this chapter to help you know your calling in life.

Let's pray together for the Lord to reveal your calling to you: "Dear Abba Father, reveal clearly to us the calling that you've placed on our lives, and help us to cultivate the related gifts you've placed in us. We desire to serve you effectively in that ministry so that we may stand before Jesus' throne during the judgment and confidently proclaim like the first servant in the Parable of the Minas: "Lord, your mina has made ten more minas!". In Jesus' name we pray, Amen!"

Fulfilling your Calling like a Competitive Athlete

"Don't you know that those who run in a race all run, but one receives the prize? Run like that, that you may win. Every man who strives in the games exercises self-control in all things. Now they do it to receive a corruptible crown, but we an incorruptible. I therefore run like that, not aimlessly. I fight like that, not beating the air, but I beat my body and bring it into submission, lest by any means, after I have preached to others, I myself should be rejected." (1 CORINTHIANS 9:24-27 WEB)

Do you now know what God has called you to do in this lifetime? For me, I believe that my calling in life is to write to influence people for the glory of God. Have you ever been in a competitive sport or activity? I've never been in a competitive sports team but I've been in a top school band and won two "gold with honors" awards at a prestigious national competition before. I played the alto saxophone. The way we trained in band was not just to have fun, but it was to win competitions. I remember we would have long practice sessions, band camps to further refine our skills, and the school hired the best conductor and coaches they could get to help us win awards. That experience helps me relate to what Paul wrote in the passage on the previous page.

Once we have identified our calling in life, we must use the gifts that we've received from God to fulfill that calling with an excellent spirit. We must do so like a competitive athlete who's training to win competitions, and not just for fun or to pass time. That means that when we do what's in our calling, we should do it without compromising on the standard of our work. We should aim to do it such that it brings glory to the Lord. It's more of a mindset than anything: Being focused on fulfilling our calling with our eyes fixed on the rewards that await us, not just the eternal ones waiting in heaven, but also the rewards here on earth. Our God is a Rewarder of people who have faith in Him.

"Without faith it is impossible to be well pleasing to him, for he who comes to God must believe that he exists, and that he is a rewarder of those who seek him." (Hebrews 11:6 WEB)

On top of that, from what I know, competitive athletes are always looking to improve their skills to get better results than they did before: They want to keep progressing - reaching new levels without ever stagnating or worse, deteriorating in their skills. Similarly, in the area you're gifted in and called to, always seek to grow in the gift and pray for God to help you to improve in your skills and techniques. He will even send people into your life to help you grow in the area you're gifted in. Hone and refine your gifts so that you can be better equipped to win your race! Here's an example: for me to grow in my gift and calling would be to practice writing a lot of new content, and to pray for improvement in my writing skills. I could get mentors or people who have the skills that I desire to train, critique or teach me. I can also keep learning new ways to increase the reach of my writing so that I can impact an even wider audience than my current one. There's so many possibilities and I know that growing in my gift is a never-ending journey as long as I am still alive on earth. Let's live life with a new level of focus to fulfill the calling that God has placed in our hearts. Our lives as believers have a divine purpose and nothing beats living a purpose-driven life - to wake up each day and know that your existence on this earth has meaning. Let's see what Paul wrote to Timothy, his disciple in Christ.

"But you be sober in all things, suffer hardship, do the work of an evangelist, and fulfill your ministry. For I am already being offered, and the time of my departure has come. I have fought the good fight. I have finished the course. I have kept the faith. From now on, the crown of righteousness is stored up for me, which the Lord, the righteous judge, will give to me on that day; and not to me only, but also to all those who have loved his appearing." (2 TIMOTHY 4:5-8 WEB)

Paul was approaching the end of his life on earth. I want to fulfill my calling such that I have the bold confidence to declare as he did: " I have fought the good and worthy and noble fight, I have finished the race, I have kept the faith".

Let's pray together: "Dear Abba Father, guide us in using the gifts to fulfill our calling with an excellent spirit and the laser-like focus of a competitive athlete. At the end of our lives on earth, we want to have the faith to confidently proclaim that we have won and finished the race. In the meantime, we want to live with an eternity-focus and we look forward to the eternal rewards that are currently waiting for us in heaven. In Jesus' name we pray, Amen!"

Parting Words

Thanks for reading this revelation - All glory goes to our Lord Jesus Christ! Here is one last passage to encourage you and for you to keep in your heart, to sustain you at all times.

"Don't be deceived. God is not mocked, for whatever a man sows, that he will also reap. For he who sows to his own flesh will from the flesh reap corruption. But he who sows to the Spirit will from the Spirit reap eternal life. Let's not be weary in doing good, for we will reap in due season, if we don't give up. So then, as we have opportunity, let's do what is good toward all men, and especially toward those who are of the household of the faith." (GALATIANS 6:7-10 WEB)

Yes, it may not be visible now and maybe there's no physical evidence that your works will bear fruit, but you can trust in the unshakable nature of God's word – you will definitely receive great rewards, so don't give up! Remember to keep overcoming evil with good, and don't ever let the world drag you down to their way of living and believing. You are the light of the world and the salt of the earth.

If you were blessed by this book, kindly send me a testimony by email to miltongoh1993@gmail.com

You can also read my blog for more new content at http://miltongoh.net

If the Holy Spirit leads you to do so, you can support my ministry by joining us as a patron at http://patreon.com/miltongohblog where you will receive exclusive rewards like more eBooks, sermon notes, original devotionals, and be part of an amazing community of Bible-believing, revelation-seeking Christians!

Made in the USA
Middletown, DE
11 December 2018